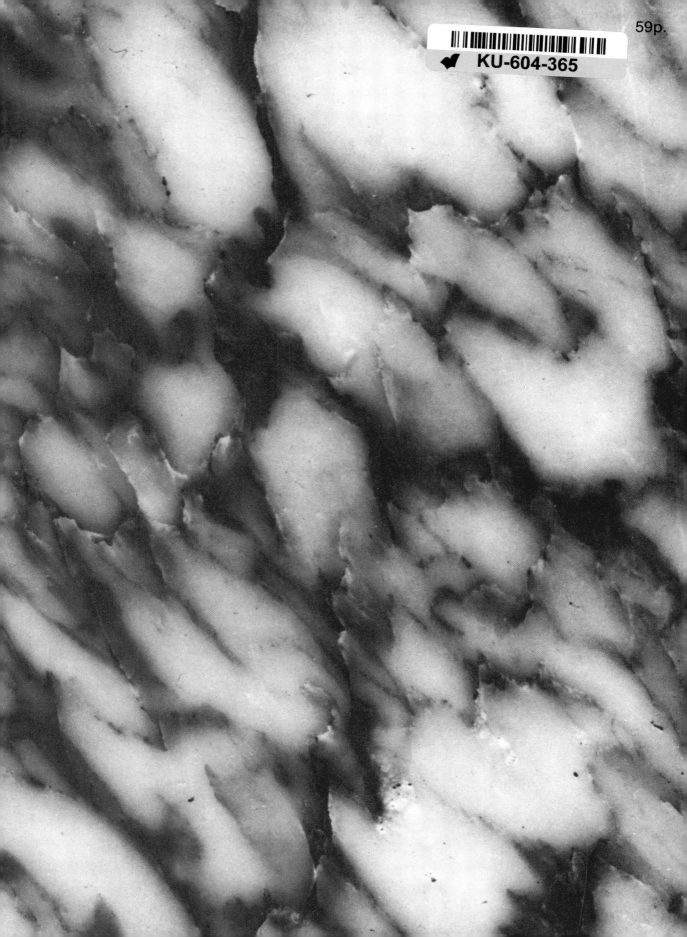

New Junior Encyclopedia

News Publishers Ltd.

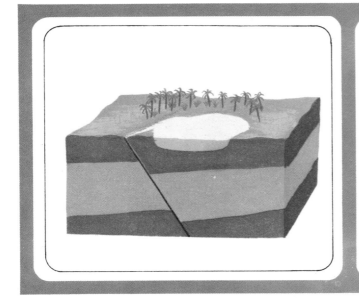

Contributors

NEIL ARDLEY B.SC.
A. L. BARRETT
N. S. BARRETT M.A.
CAROLE BERKSON
LUCY BERMAN B.A.
A. S. BUTTERFIELD
RONALD L. CARTER B.SC.(ECON), F.R.G.S.
ANN CLARK
JOHN O. E. CLARK B.SC., A.R.I.C.
J. N. CLEAVER M.A.
T. G. COOK M.A.
JEAN COOKE
TOM EDWARDS
JILL R. GIRLING B.A.
PETER GREY
R. J. W. HAMMOND
BRENDAN HENNESSY
L. JAMES M.A., PH.D.
ROBIN KERROD
ANN KRAMER
JO LOGAN
K. E. LOWTHER M.A.
KEITH LYE B.A., F.R.G.S.
L. H. MUNBY M.A.
DOMINIC RECALDIN B.SC., PH.D.

THEODORE ROWLAND-ENTWISTLE F.R.G.S.
G. E. SATTERTHWAITE F.R.A.S.
D. S. SEHBAI M.A.
D. SHARP L.R.A.M.
G. M. WESTON B.A.
B. G. WILSON
MICHAEL E. WRIGHT B.A.

© 1974 Macdonald & Co (Publishers) Ltd, London.
Distributed in U.K. by arrangement with
City Magazines, 1-3 Wine Office Court, Fleet Street, London.
Distributed in Australia and New Zealand by
Bay Books (Pty) Ltd, Sydney.
Made and printed in Great Britain by
Purnell & Sons Ltd, Paulton.

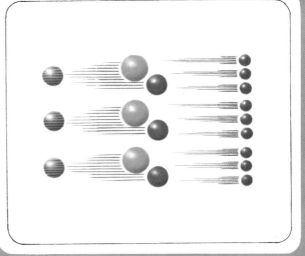

Harvesting dates from
a palm grove

Jawaharlal Nehru, Indian Prime Minister for 17 years.

Nehru, Jawaharlal (1889-1964), was India's first prime minister after the country gained independence in 1947. He held that office until his death, 17 years later. Nehru was born in Allahabad, and was educated and trained as a lawyer in England. After returning to India, he joined his father in national politics. Nehru became a close friend and disciple of Mohandas K. Gandhi, India's great leader in the movement against British rule through passive resistance. For his political activities, Nehru spent more than 10 years in prison.

As prime minister, Nehru improved economic and social conditions in his country. He was greatly admired by the people. In international affairs, he became a spokesman for African and Asian nations. He followed a policy of neutrality—avoiding alliances with either the Communist or Western countries. Two years after Nehru's death, his daughter, Mrs Indira P. Gandhi, became prime minister.

Nelson, Horatio (1758-1805), a British admiral, was one of the greatest seamen in history. His brilliant victories in several battles against the French made Britain a great sea power and crippled Napoleon's empire in Europe. He was a great leader because both the ordinary seamen and his officers trusted him and were trusted by him.

Nelson, the son of a rector, was born at the parsonage of Burnham Thorpe in Norfolk. He went to sea as a boy, soon deciding that he would be a hero. So rapid was his promotion that he was a post captain by the age of twenty. From 1793 onwards he was fighting the French and Spanish in the Mediterranean. For his outstanding tactics at the Battle of Cape St Vincent, 1797, under Admiral Jervis, he was acclaimed a hero by his countrymen. A wound made him blind in one eye, and the following year he lost his right arm in a daring attack on Santa Cruz de Tenerife in the Canary Isles. By this time he was a rear-admiral. He chased the French all over the Mediterranean before completely defeating them at the Battle of the Nile in 1798.

Right: Portrait of Horatio Nelson in the full dress uniform of Vice-Admiral of the White Squadron.

Below: Nelson destroyed Napoleon's fleet at the Battle of the Nile in 1798. From then on the French were severely hampered by British naval superiority.

Nelson was struck down by a shot while gaining his most famous victory—at Trafalgar. As commander-in-chief of the British fleet, he had pursued the French to the West Indies and back before cornering them at Cape Trafalgar, Spain, on October 21, 1805. The beginning of the great battle was marked by Nelson's famous signal: 'England expects that every man will do his duty.' Nelson died, on his ship the *Victory*, as the battle was ending.

Above: Nelson's flagship, the *Victory*, led the British fleet at Trafalgar. It is shown here in dry dock at Portsmouth flying the famous signal: 'England expects that every man will do his duty.'

Nelson is a province of New Zealand. It covers an area of 10,312 square miles in the northwestern part of South Island. Approximately 64,300 people live there. Most of the population is concentrated in two areas: around Tasman Bay in the north, and in the so-called Buller district in the west. Several high mountain ranges cover much of the rest of the province. The Nelson Lakes National Park is a favourite region for camping, boating and fishing.

Near Tasman Bay, the land is low-lying, with a mild and sunny climate. Farming is a major activity in this region. Apples,

Haulashore Island, in Nelson Province New Zealand.

hops, tobacco and vegetables are grown in large quantities. This produce is canned or processed and shipped from Nelson, the chief city of the northern region and the provincial capital. Coal mining is the main activity in the Buller district. Westport is the largest city and port there.

Abel Tasman, the Dutch navigator, first sailed into Tasman Bay in 1642. Two hundred years later, an official settlement was started at Nelson.

Nelson River flows for about 400 miles through the province of Manitoba in Canada. It is the principal river of the province. The Nelson forms part of a 1,600-mile-long waterway that begins at the Saskatchewan River and ends at Hudson Bay.

The Nelson itself has its source at the north end of Lake Winnipeg. It flows in a north-eastward direction. It crosses Lakes Playgreen, Cross, and Split. It enters Hudson Bay at Port Nelson.

Fur trappers in the region used the Nelson as their major transport route. For many years the Hudson's Bay Company dominated the region. Today, the power stations on the Nelson provide hydro-electric power for the province's industries and homes.

Nepal is a Hindu country in central Asia. It is ruled by a king. Katmandu is the capital and only large city. Nepal has an area of 54,362 square miles. It is surrounded by land on all sides. Tibet, Sikkim, and India are its neighbours.

Nepal is a mountainous country. The world's highest peak—Mount Everest, 29,028 feet—lies in the Himalaya Mountains which occupy the north. Jungles and swamps are part of Nepal's landscape. The fertile Nepal Valley occupies the centre.

Nepal has 11,247,616 inhabitants. Farming is the main occupation. Rice, wheat and fruit are grown. There are only a few light industries, such as handicrafts made at home.

Left: The map shows the location of the mountain kingdom of Nepal (marked in black). Above: A street scene in Katmandu, Nepal's capital and largest city. In the foreground, a porter brings wares from the countryside, and a pig searches for food.

Neptune Counting outwards from the Sun, Neptune is the eighth planet of the Solar System. It was discovered because irregular movements of Uranus led astronomers to suspect the presence of another planet nearby. They searched the probable area and eventually found Neptune in 1846.

Neptune is nearly 28,000 miles across. It is on average 2,794 million miles from the Sun, and takes 165 years to travel round it. The temperature on Neptune is

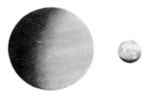

Above: Neptune compared in size with the Earth. It is nearly 28,000 miles across.

Below: Through a telescope Neptune appears as a small greenish disc with lighter bands running across it.

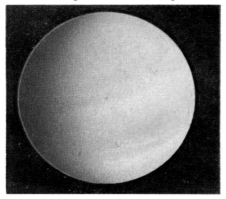

very low—about minus 200° C. Its atmosphere is a mixture of poisonous gases, probably about 2,000 miles deep. Neptune has two moons, Triton and Nereid.

Nero (A.D. 37-68) was a Roman emperor, famed for his cruelty and corruption. His full name was Nero Claudius Caesar Drusus Germanicus. He became emperor in 54, succeeding his stepfather Claudius.

Nero was a talented singer, actor and poet. But he is known to have murdered many people, including his mother, his first wife, and Claudius's son Britannicus. He blamed the great fire of Rome in 64, which some people think he started, on the Christians and began a merciless persecution of them. But finally, in 68, the army rose against him. Nero fled and committed suicide.

Nervous system, in man and the higher animals, consists of the brain, the spinal cord and the nerves that run to all the bodily organs.

The brain and the spinal cord together are known as the *central nervous system*. The nerves that extend to all parts of the body are the *peripheral nervous system*.

One of the most important functions of the body's nervous system is to help us to gain information about our surroundings, and about changes inside our bodies, so that we can take whatever actions are needed for our well-being. This information is gathered by the sense organs—such as the organs of sight, taste and touch—and passes as a stream of signals through the *sensory nerves* to the spinal cord and the brain. The brain may store it or, if some action is necessary, may send a 'message' through the *motor nerves* to muscles that make the needed response. For example, if we look at a bright light, we respond by closing our eyes. That is to say, the stimulus of the light has resulted in a 'message' being passed along sensory nerves to our brain that our eyes find the light intolerable. To protect our eyes, our brain, through motor nerves, activates the muscles that close our eye-lids.

Some nerves regulate activities of our body that are necessary for life but over which we have no conscious control—for

The Emperor Nero is often blamed for the great fire of Rome in AD 64. He is renowned for his cruelty.

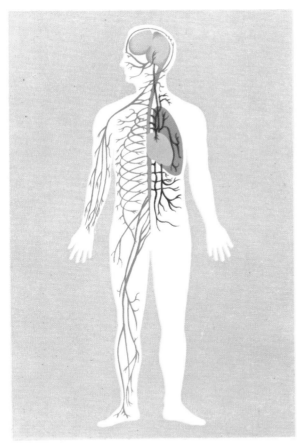

The central nervous system (brains and spinal cord) is brown. Nerves that pass to the skin (sensory) and muscles (motor) are in red; the purple nerves pass to structures inside your body and you cannot control them. Of course both sensory and motor nerves spread all through your body.

example, the working of our heart, lungs or digestive system. These nerves are called the *autonomic nervous system.*

The body automatically responds to certain stimuli without the brain having to determine what action is necessary. A response of this kind is called a *reflex action.* As an example, if we touch a hot cooker, our hand immediately jerks back.

Most of the nervous system is made up of nerve cells called *neurons.* As with other cells, each neuron has a cell body of a nucleus surrounded by cytoplasm. Tiny branches of threads called *dendrites* grow out from the cell body and make connections with neighbouring neurons. The cells do not actually touch each other, but the nervous impulses can easily 'jump' across the gap. As well as the dendrites many neurons have a much longer branch called an *axon* or *nerve fibre.* These axons are very fine, but they may be several feet long. The nerves which run to all parts of our bodies consist mainly of axons.

When the dendrites of a neuron receive a stimulus or signal, an impulse passes along them to the cell body and then to the axon. The axon carries the signal to the dendrites of the next neuron (which passes it on in the same way) or to an *effector organ,* such as a muscle cell, which makes the body's response to the stimulus. An axon can normally carry a signal in one direction only, so we have sensory and effector nerve fibres, carrying signals to and from the brain respectively. A nerve, such as that running along an arm, generally has both kinds of fibres in it, each insulated from its neighbours by a fatty sheath.

Netherlands The Netherlands is a small, low-lying country in western Europe. For its size, more people live there than in any other country—about 920 per square mile. The country is sometimes called Holland, and its people are known as Dutch.

The Netherlands is bounded on the north-west by the North Sea, on the east by Germany, and on the south by Belgium. It lies at the mouths of the Rhine, Maas (Meuse) and Scheldt (Schelde) rivers. Much of the land has been built up by silt dropped by the rivers where they enter the sea.

Nearly half the country is *polder* land —that is, land that has been reclaimed from the sea. Two-thirds of the polder land is below sea-level. It is protected from the sea by sand-dunes and *dykes,* great banks built by the Dutch. The rest of the country is above sea-level, but the highest point is less than 350 feet.

The people speak Dutch, a language similar to German. Many Dutch people are tall, fair-haired and blue-eyed.

Facts and Figures
Area: 15,785 square miles.
Population: 13,119,000.
Capital: Amsterdam.
Money Unit: guilder.
Labour force: 55% urban,
45% rural.
Exports: bulbs, dairy
products, ships, textiles.
Imports: coffee, petro-
leum, tin, sugar.

Right: Cheeses and flower
bulbs are among the
Netherlands' chief exports.
Below: The Netherlands is
famous for its picturesque
windmills.

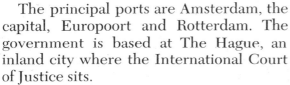

The principal ports are Amsterdam, the capital, Europoort and Rotterdam. The government is based at The Hague, an inland city where the International Court of Justice sits.

Agriculture is very important since nearly all of the soil is rich and fertile. Dairying is more important than crop growing and the country exports large quantities of butter and cheese. Almost as important is the growing of tulip, hyacinth and other flower bulbs in the area around Haarlem.

Apart from petroleum and natural gas, the country has few natural resources. Dutch industries process food or other agricultural products, such as flax and sugar. Engineering and chemical industries are also important. International trade passing through its ports to other European lands contributes to the Netherlands' wealth. Some goods travel along the network of canals that covers the country.

For hundreds of years the Netherlands and Belgium were linked together. They were often known as the Low Countries. The area came under the rule of Spain in the early 1500's. However, in 1562 the people of the Netherlands, led by William, Prince of Orange, rebelled against Spain, and formed a republic. War with Spain lasted until 1648.

The French conquered the Netherlands in 1795, but the country regained its independence in 1815, after the Napoleonic Wars. The Germans occupied the Netherlands from 1940 to 1945, during World War II. In 1957, the country joined the European Common Market, a trade alliance with five other countries.

Nevada is a thinly populated state in the western United States. It has only 489,000 people. Nevada is so dry that on much of the land only desert sagebrush grows. But beneath the ground there are rich deposits of copper, gold and other minerals which make mining a leading

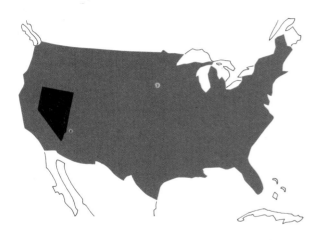

This map shows the location of Nevada.

activity. Tourists also bring revenue to the state. The gambling resorts at Las Vegas and Reno are world famous. Visitors also come to see ghost towns, such as Virginia City, that were once busy mining centres. Cattle and sheep ranching are the most important agricultural activities, while hay and other crops for animal feed are grown. Carson City is the state capital.

The United States acquired Nevada from Mexico after the Mexican War of 1846-1848. The discovery of silver at Comstock Lode in 1859 brought many settlers. Nevada became a state in 1864. When the price of silver fell in the 1870's and 1880's many people left. Since 1950 the United States government has used areas in Nevada for testing atomic weapons.

New Brunswick is a province in eastern Canada. It was one of the country's four original provinces.

New Brunswick borders on Quebec and Nova Scotia, and on the state of Maine in the United States. It has about 500 miles of coastline on the Gulf of St. Lawrence and the Bay of Fundy. Both of these are arms of the Atlantic Ocean. The coast provides many good harbours.

The province has an area of 28,354 square miles. Most of it is forested. The land is hilly. There are many valleys cut by rushing rivers, the largest of which is the St. John. The rivers provide hydro-electric power. They are also used for floating millions of logs to processing plants. New Brunswick's weather is cold in winter and warm in summer.

About half of New Brunswick's 623,000 inhabitants live in cities. Saint John, the largest city, is a manufacturing and shipping centre. Fredericton is the provincial capital.

New Brunswick's industries depend upon the rich natural resources of the province. The forests yield wood, much of which is used for making paper. Coal, copper, lead, silver and zinc are mined. Fishermen take lobsters, cod, flounder and sardines from the surrounding waters.

New Brunswick's farmers grow potatoes, oats, barley and apples. Dairy farming and poultry farming are also important.

French fur traders settled in the New Brunswick region in the 1600's. They called it *Acadia*. The British took the region in 1755, during the French and Indian Wars.

After the American War of Independence New Brunswick gained thousands of new settlers. These were people who left the United States because they remained loyal to Britain.

This map shows the location of New Brunswick.

Newfoundland is a province of Canada. Its island territories were once an independent dominion (see Canada). The province consists of the island of Newfoundland, off the Atlantic coast of Can-

The fishing village at Petty Harbor, Newfoundland. Fishing is an important industry of the province.

ada and Labrador, part of the Canadian mainland. The total area is 156,185 square miles.

The coast of the island is rocky, with many deep inlets. The central part is a rugged plateau, with many lakes and forests. The forests provide timber for wood-pulp and paper-making, one of Newfoundland's main industries. The island is rich in minerals, including

This map shows the location of Newfoundland.

gypsum, iron ore, lead and zinc. Only a small amount of land around the coast can be farmed. The climate is cool, with several months of heavy snow in winter.

Labrador consists of a plateau sloping steeply to the coast, which has many *fiords* (deep sea inlets). Only about 20,000 of Newfoundland's 517,000 people live in Labrador. About one-third of the land is covered with forests. In the north-west lies one of the world's richest deposits of iron ore. The climate is generally colder than that of Newfoundland.

Fishing is one of the province's main industries. Near the island lie shallow areas of sea known as the Banks, where there is abundant food for fish. About 200 million cod are caught there every year. St. John's, Newfoundland's capital, is the base for the fishing fleet.

Newfoundland was Britain's oldest colony. It was claimed in 1583. It became self-governing in 1855, but after an economic crisis, sought help from Britain in 1934. It joined Canada in 1949.

New Guinea, one of the world's largest islands, lies in the tropics north of Australia. The western part of the island, West Irian, is part of Indonesia. Eastern New Guinea is divided into Papua and the United Nations Trust Territory of New Guinea, which are both governed by Australia.

New Guinea has an area of 317,115 square miles. As an island, it is second only to Greenland in size.

The island has a 'backbone' of mountains from west to east. The mountains slope southwards to the southern plain, the western part of which is a tropical swamp. Except in the mountains, New Guinea is unpleasantly hot and humid. Forests cover much of the island.

The climate and physical features have made life difficult for the people of New Guinea and delayed the development of the island.

The population of New Guinea is about 2,500,000. Melanesian, Micronesian, Poly-

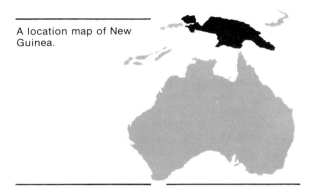

A location map of New Guinea.

nesian and pygmy people live on the island. The principal cities are Port Moresby and Sukarnapura, but they are both small.

About 700 languages and dialects are spoken and many religions practised. Some islanders are Christians. Some follow a cult that was inspired by the islanders' experiences in World War II, called the *Cargo Cult*. They wait for the return of huge birds (aircraft) to drop from the skies all the goods that the islanders want to possess. They believe that Euro-

New Guinea

Right: Native tribes from New Guinea and Papua prepare to enter the arena at the Mount Hagan show

Below: A native woman and a warrior picking coffee berries on a plantation in New Guinea. The beans are fermented in concrete vats to get rid of the red skin and then dried before being exported.

Below right: Barakau, a village built on stilts on the Papuan coast at the south-east corner of New Guinea.

peans will then leave New Guinea, but leave their goods behind, as often happened during the war. Some of the tribes living in the jungle of the interior are very primitive. Their way of life is similar to that of the early inhabitants of Europe in the Stone Age.

Spanish sailors landed in northern New Guinea in 1526. In 1660, the Dutch occupied part of western New Guinea. By the late 1880's, Britain and Germany shared the eastern part of the island. By 1920 Australia governed all eastern New Guinea. Northern New Guinea was occupied by the Japanese during World War II, and fierce fighting took place there. The Dutch handed over western New Guinea to Indonesia in 1963.

New Hampshire, a state in New England, has some of the most beautiful scenery in the United States. Forests cover much of its area, there are numerous lakes and quiet valleys. In the north, New Hampshire has the rugged grandeur of the White Mountains. Each year thousands of holiday-makers from the large northeastern cities, many of them hikers or campers, visit the state. New Hampshire

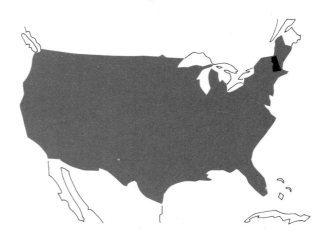

This map shows the location of New Hampshire.

is also popular with skiers, who flock to the mountain ski resorts in winter. The population of the state is 738,000.

There is little farming in the rocky soil of New Hampshire, and most of the state's income comes from manufacturing. The leather industry has long been important. Engineering and chemical industries are growing rapidly. Portsmouth, on the Atlantic coast, has a major shipyard. Manchester is the busiest industrial city, and Concord is the state capital.

New Hampshire is famous for the town

Snow-covered countryside in New Hampshire. Many people visit this state for its skiing and for the brilliant forest colours in autumn.

934

meetings held in its villages and small towns. All the people of each town have the right to attend an annual meeting and help to make decisions on local affairs. New Hampshire's first settlers, in the early 1600's, led hard lives, struggling against the bitter winters and hostile Indians. The colony was the first to declare independence from Britain in 1776.

New Jersey is the most densely populated state in the United States, with 7,168,000 people living in an area of less than 8,000 square miles. It lies on the Atlantic coast between the two huge cities of New York and Philadelphia. Many people who work in these cities commute daily from their homes in New Jersey. The state has many important industrial towns, and has ocean ports at Hoboken and Newark. Newark Airport is one of the busiest airports in the United States. The state capital is Trenton.

New Jersey is chiefly a manufacturing state. Many companies are attracted to it by its favourable tax laws. Chemicals, machinery and processed food are major products. There are many prosperous small farms and fishermen make valuable catches of shellfish. Large numbers of holidaymakers visit Atlantic City and other popular coast resorts.

New Jersey was settled by the Dutch as part of New Netherland. Later, it became

The remains of an Indian village sheltering under cliffs in New Mexico.

one of the 13 English colonies. Several battles of the American War of Independence took place there.

New Mexico, one of the most thinly populated states of the United States, lies on the Mexican border. Its 1,016,000 people include many Indians living on reservations. New Mexico has wide plains, deserts, mountains and great canyons. The Rio Grande flows through it, providing irrigation for a large area. The state capital is Santa Fe, but the largest city is Albuquerque.

Mining and farming are the state's leading industries. The chief mineral products are oil and natural gas, but New Mexico also has valuable deposits of uranium and potash. In many parts of the state there are large ranches where sheep and cattle graze. Cotton and wheat are among the crops grown.

Remains of ancient settlements show

This map shows the location of New Jersey.

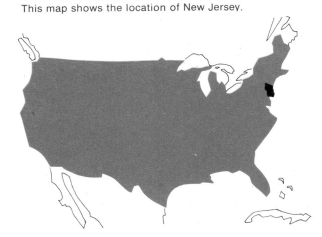

935

Ornamental ironwork is a feature of the old houses in New Orleans. Many of the people of this city still speak French.

that Indian civilizations existed in what is now New Mexico thousands of years before European navigators reached the Americas. Spanish explorers claimed the region for Spain in the 1500's. In the 1800's New Mexico became a province of Mexico. The United States took the region in the Mexican War of 1846-1848, and New Mexico became the 47th state in 1912. Mexican and Spanish influence is still apparent in New Mexico today.

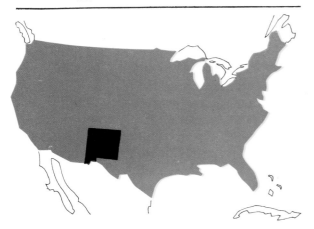

This map shows the location of New Mexico.

New Orleans (pop. 593,000) is a city, seaport, and former capital of the State of Louisiana, U.S.A. It is situated on low-lying marshland on the Mississippi, 107 miles from the river mouth on the Gulf of Mexico. A series of *levees* (embankments) are a feature of the riverside as a protection against flood. It is the largest city of Louisiana and the chief commercial centre of the Gulf States.

New Orleans was founded in 1718 by the French under Bienville, and has risen to become the great cotton market of America and one of the foremost cotton ports of the world.

New South Wales is a state in the south-eastern part of Australia. It has 4,623,900 people — more than any other state in the country. It is also the richest state in terms of industrial and agricultural production. The Australian Capital

A location map of New South Wales.

Territory, lying within New South Wales, was given by the state to the federal government in 1911 as the site of the nation's capital.

New South Wales covers an area of 309,433 square miles. On the east it has a coastline on the Pacific Ocean. On the south it is bounded by Victoria across the Murray River; on the west by South Australia; and on the north by Queensland. The principal rivers in the state are the Murray and Darling, and their tributaries, the Murrumbidgee and Lachlan. The rivers are important for irrigation and hydroelectric power.

The state has four main regions. In the east is a narrow coastal region, which is low-lying and has much fertile land. Farmers in this region cultivate sugarcane and fruit, and raise dairy cattle. There are rich deposits of coal. Farther inland, the terrain rises to the Tableland of the Great Dividing Range, a region of mixed crop and livestock farming. Beyond this are the Western Slopes, primarily a region of wheat-growing and sheep-raising. In the extreme west are the vast, dry Western Plains where sheep grazing is the only profitable form of agriculture.

The coast of New South Wales was the first area to be settled. Today, it still has the greatest concentration of people and industries. Sydney, the state capital and Australia's largest city, is located on the coast and has a busy harbour. From it thousands of tons of wool, wheat, fruit, dairy products and meat are exported each year. Sydney's factories produce chemicals, woollen and synthetic textiles, cars, electrical goods and processed foods. North of Sydney is Newcastle, a prosperous port and manufacturing centre, and south of it is Wollongong. Coalfields near these two cities supply fuel for a productive steel industry.

New South Wales has valuable deposits

The Blue Mountains of New South Wales were given their name because they often appear in a bluish haze. This is caused by tiny drops of eucalyptus oil in the atmosphere.

of lead, zinc and silver in the west, particularly near Broken Hill. The state has extensive forests, which produce both hard and softwood timber. In the state's coastal waters, fishermen catch tuna for canning and a variety of shellfish.

Captain James Cook was the first explorer to reach the east coast of Australia, in 1770. He gave the region the name New South Wales but included territory that is no longer part of the state. Tasmania, South Australia, Victoria and Queensland were carved out of New South Wales between 1825 and 1859.

In 1788, Captain Arthur Phillip established the first formal settlement at Sydney with a group of English convicts. People transported from Britain continued to make up a sizeable proportion of the population until 1852. In the early days the population also included many soldiers and their families. The introduction of merino sheep for the wool industry attracted a new wave of settlers, and with the opening up of the Western Plains after 1813 the wool industry flourished. Gold brought still more settlers to the state in the 1850's. In 1855 New South Wales became self-governing and in 1901 became part of the Commonwealth of Australia.

Newspapers provide us with news and comment and articles of interest every day. Serious or *quality* newspapers, such as *The Times* in Britain and *The New York Times* in the United States, appeal to informed people by concentrating on politics and business news. *Popular* papers, for example, the British *Sun,* appeal to a larger proportion of newspaper readers by having an entertaining style and an emphasis on 'human' stories about incidents that happen to people.

These papers are daily or evening papers, published every morning or evening in a superbly organized rush of activity. On Sundays, special newspapers appear that are more concerned with feature articles and comment than with news.

They may contain various supplements devoted to special subjects. The Sunday edition of *The New York Times* comes in a dozen sections and contains over 600 pages altogether! But most of the paper consists of advertisements. Almost all papers depend on advertisements to keep them going. If it were not for advertisements, newspapers would cost twice their present price or more.

In most countries, newspapers serve small areas around cities. In Australia, for example, most of the newspapers are local and circulate in the areas around the big cities. These include *The Adelaide Advertiser, The Sydney Morning Herald* and *The Melbourne Herald.* There is one national newspaper — *The Australian.* But in Britain and Russia, newspapers are read nationally. Britain has eight national daily newspapers and Russia two. One of

The front page of the London *Times* of 7th November, 1805, containing the news of the victory at Trafalgar. When it first appeared, the *Times* was known as 'The Thunderer' because of the violent tone of its articles.

Russia's, *Pravda* (meaning *truth*), has one of the largest sales of any newspaper—about five million copies a day. At the other end of the scale, local weekly newspapers serve small towns, featuring only local news.

In some countries, such as Spain, Greece and Russia, newspapers are controlled by governments. In others, a newspaper may print what it likes but many often support a political party.

Talking points
* Most newspapers contain a high proportion of advertisements. Why do you think that they have this?
* As well as reporting the news, some newspapers give support to a political party. Do you prefer to read an independent paper or one that has a political bias?
* Newspapers publish home news, foreign news, sports news, business news and features on interesting subjects. Which do you turn to first?

Articles to read
Communications; Printing.

Newts are amphibian animals which can live both in fresh water and on the land. Newts have long tails to swim with and four short legs to move about on land. A newt is also called an *eft*. Newts are related to salamanders, and, like salamanders, many newts are brightly coloured. (See Amphibians.)

Newts are cold-blooded animals and hibernate through the winter. They breed in the spring, laying eggs singly on water plants in ponds. The eggs hatch to form tadpoles. These develop like the

Sir Isaac Newton after a portrait by Sir Godfrey Kneller.

tadpoles of frogs except that the newt tadpole does not lose its tail (see Frog). Some newt tadpoles never leave the water, and breed without reaching complete adulthood. Most newts spend much time in the water. Like frogs, they can breathe by absorbing oxygen from the water through their skin. But in the summer they usually leave the water to live in moist places on the land.

Newts grow to a length of about three to six inches. They are unusual in that they can grow new legs to replace any they lose.

Newton, Sir Isaac (1642-1727), was an English mathematician who made outstanding contributions to the study of physics. His theories of gravity and motion and experiments in light physics have earned him a place among the most celebrated of scientists.

As a boy he was not a notable scholar. Neither did he show great ability while studying at Trinity College, Cambridge. However his greatest discoveries were

A male Smooth Newt (above), and a female Warty Newt (below).

made during a period of only two years, soon after leaving college.

Newton proved that sunlight is made up of all the colours of the rainbow. He demonstrated this by passing sunlight through a *prism* (a triangular block of glass) onto a piece of paper. This resulted in the *spectrum,* or band of colours, being clearly seen. To prove conclusively that his theory was correct, Newton then passed the spectrum back through another prism and obtained white light again. Although similar theories had previously been put forward, it was Newton who proved it beyond doubt.

It is popularly believed that Newton's theories of motion and gravity came to him when he saw an apple fall from a tree to the ground beneath. Gravity is the attraction that masses of matter have for each other, and motion occurs when an object changes its position in space. Newton reasoned that the force with which the Earth attracts an object depends on the amount of *matter* (of which all physical things are made) in the object, and the distance between them. Therefore a large stone will be attracted to Earth by a greater force than a small stone. Newton also concluded that the planets are held in their orbits by the gravitational pull of the Sun, while the Moon is held in its orbit by the Earth's gravitational pull.

It was nearly twenty years later that Newton's theories were published. The resulting book is considered one of the most important scientific works. His work on the laws of motion became the basis for the science of mechanics.

Newton had an extremely busy academic and public life. In 1669 he was appointed professor of mathematics at Cambridge, and later became the university's member of parliament. He was made Master of the Mint in 1699 and organized the issue of new coinage. He became president of the Royal Society in 1703 and held the post until his death. Newton was knighted by Queen Anne in 1705.

New York City is a city and seaport of the state of New York, in the United States. It is situated on four islands and a part of the mainland at the mouth of the Hudson (or North) River at the head of New York Bay.

Originally a small Dutch settlement at the southern tip of Manhattan Island, the city now incorporates the five boroughs of Manhattan, Brooklyn, Queens, Richmond (Staten Island), and Bronx (mainland). With a population of 7,895,000, it is the largest city in the western hemisphere and after Tokyo and London the third largest in the world. Huge bridges and long tunnels crossing the Hudson and East Rivers are of major importance in the city's communications.

It is the chief commercial centre of the United States, with Manhattan the commercial and financial heart of the city. Mammoth skyscrapers are a feature of the city. The Empire State Building is a gigantic office complex. It was the world's tallest building, with 102 storeys and an overall height of 1,472 feet but is now surpassed by the World Trade Centre (1,718 feet) in Manhattan. The New York Stock Exchange (Wall Street) is the greatest securities market in the world. The city is the headquarters of many industrial concerns, and major industries include textiles, publishing, iron and steel works, machinery manufacture, sugar refining and chemical products.

New York is the principal port of America. The west side of Manhattan Island on the Hudson River is lined with docks and port facilities, and there are also important docks at Brooklyn. One of the largest harbours in the world, it carries more than half the total foreign trade of the United States. The waters of the Hudson River, East River, Long Island Sound, and the Harlem River are used

The Statue of Liberty stands at the entrance to New York harbour on Liberty Island. From the base of the plinth to the top of the torch it measures over 300 feet. It was presented to the United States by France in 1884 as a symbol of friendship.

New York. The United Nations building (right foreground).

extensively by small freighter and barge traffic.

The city is an important educational and cultural centre and is the seat of Columbia University (founded 1754), of the New York University (1831) and of many other academic institutions.

New York is a state in the north-east of the United States. It has 18,191,000 inhabitants, and, except for California, is the most highly populated state in the country. Most of its people live in cities and towns. More than half of them live in or around New York City, the largest city in the United States and one of the largest in the world. Buffalo, Rochester and Albany, the state capital, are among the state's other large cities.

New York state is the financial, industrial and commercial centre of the United States and has been so for over 100 years. Its most important industries include the manufacture of clothing and machinery, food processing and publishing and printing. The harbour of New York City is the country's leading seaport. Buffalo, an inland port on Lake Erie, has grown in importance since the opening of the St. Lawrence Seaway in 1959.

Agriculture is also highly developed in New York. The state has broad pasture lands for raising dairy cattle. Poultry

This map shows the location of New York State.

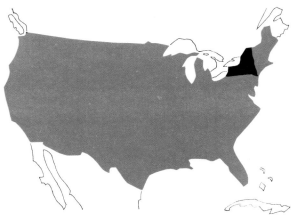

farming and market gardening are important too.

Many tourists visit New York state. Some are attracted by the sights of New York City, but others come to enjoy camping, skiing and climbing in the Adirondack and Catskill mountains. Niagara Falls in the west is especially popular with honeymooners. Long Island has miles of fine Atlantic Ocean beaches.

New York was first claimed for the Netherlands by the English navigator Henry Hudson in 1609. The Dutch named it New Netherland. When the English took over in 1664, they changed its name to New York, in honour of the Duke of York. After the American War of Independence, New York City served as the nation's capital until 1790.

New Zealand is a country over 1,000 miles south-east of Australia. Most of New Zealand is made up of two large islands, called North Island and South Island. It contains several other islands, but they

Facts and Figures
Area: 103,736 square miles.
Population: 2,955,000.
Capital: Wellington.
Money Unit: New Zealand dollar.
Labour force: 36% rural; 64% urban.
Exports: butter, cheese, meat, wool.
Imports: fuel, machinery, textiles, tools.

are very small. New Zealand is almost as big as the British Isles. More than nine-tenths of all New Zealanders were born in the British Isles, or are descended from British and Irish people who settled in New Zealand.

North Island, where two-thirds of all New Zealanders live, extends about 500 miles from north to south. Its low mountains and hills include two active volcanoes. South Island is separated from North Island by the 16-mile-wide Cook Strait. From the Strait, the Southern Alps stretch south-westwards for more than 500 miles throughout the island. New

Above: Maoris in national costume perform an action song. The Maoris inhabited New Zealand when the first settlers arrived.
Above right: The cathedral at Christchurch, in the South Island.
Far right: A climbing party negotiates an icebridge in Mt. Cook National Park. New Zealanders are fond of outdoor recreations.

Below right: Hot springs at Rotorua. This area is famous for its geysers of boiling mud pools.
Left: The kiwi is a tailless, flightless bird which is often used as a national emblem.

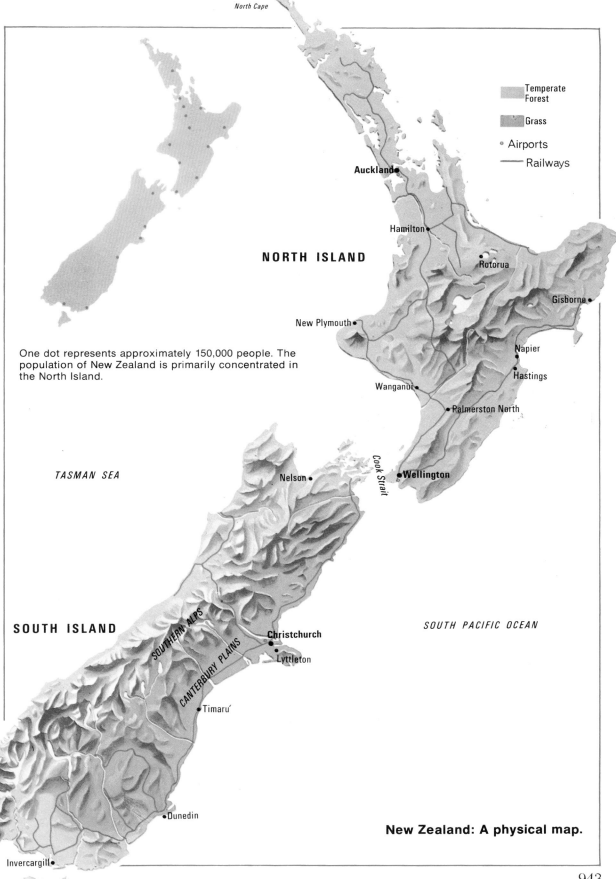

North Cape

Temperate Forest

Grass

○ Airports

—— Railways

Auckland●

Hamilton●

NORTH ISLAND

●Rotorua

●Gisborne

New Plymouth●

●Napier

●Hastings

Wanganui●

●Palmerston North

One dot represents approximately 150,000 people. The population of New Zealand is primarily concentrated in the North Island.

TASMAN SEA

Nelson●

Cook Strait

●**Wellington**

SOUTH PACIFIC OCEAN

SOUTH ISLAND

SOUTHERN ALPS

CANTERBURY PLAINS

Christchurch●

●Lyttleton

●Timaru

●Dunedin

Invercargill●

New Zealand: A physical map.

943

Sheep-farming is vital to New Zealand's economy. Wool and lamb are among its chief exports.

volcanic activity. On North Island is a region around Rotorua where hot springs and boiling mud pools are found. Some of the hot springs are *geysers*, which periodically shoot up a tall column of hot water and steam.

New Zealand has a mild climate. In January the country's mid-summer temperature averages about 68° F (20° C). In July, temperatures drop to about 42° F (6° C). Rainfall is very varied, averaging between 20 and 200 inches in various parts of the islands.

New Zealand has several species of rare birds. The tail-less kiwi is often used as a symbol for the country.

About 7 people out of every 100 are *Maoris,* who are descendants of the Polynesian people who sailed to the islands about 700 years ago. Many marriages have occurred between Maoris and Europeans. The official language of New Zealand is English, but the Maoris also have their own language. The religion of the country is Christianity.

Zealand's highest mountain, Mount Cook, rises from this range.

Many bays and beaches lie along New Zealand's 4,300-mile-long coastline. The country has several rivers. Most of them flow so swiftly down steep slopes that boats cannot use them. New Zealand has many spectacular lakes and waterfalls. In addition to active volcanoes, it has other natural features associated with

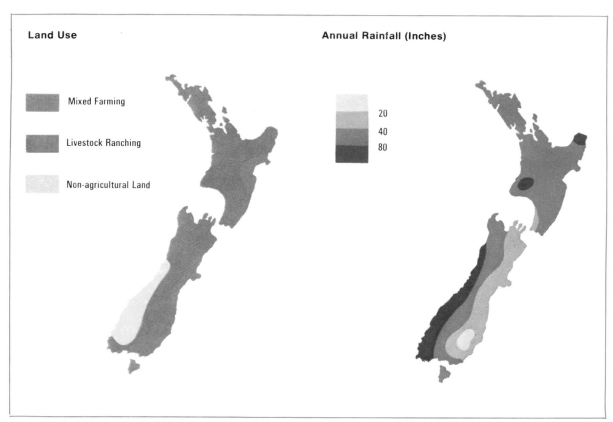

Land Use

Mixed Farming

Livestock Ranching

Non-agricultural Land

Annual Rainfall (Inches)

20
40
80

Marlborough Province, in the north-east part of New Zealand's South Island, has many hills and mountains. Its sheltered bays are much used for water skiing and yachting.

New Zealand is one of the most prosperous countries in the world. It was one of the earliest countries to introduce social reforms and a social security system, including old age pensions. The mild climate allows New Zealanders to enjoy an outdoor life in their leisure time, to a much greater extent than their parents or grandparents did in Britain. Popular recreations include athletics, cricket and rugby football. Most New Zealanders live in small towns or villages. Only Auckland, Christchurch and Wellington, the capital, have more than 100,000 people.

Half of New Zealand's area is farmland, and the country exports butter, lamb, fruit and other food products, especially to Britain. New Zealand has fertile soil. Farmers grow cereals for consumption in New Zealand. Because the most modern methods of farming are used, only a sixth of the country's people work on the land. Two-thirds of the people work in manufacturing and processing industries of various kinds. Much electrical power comes from hydro-electric plants, which harness the power of New Zealand's rush-ing rivers. The fishing industry is also important but employs few people.

Forests cover about a fifth of New Zealand. Most of the forests were planted in the 1920's. The country's mineral wealth includes coal, iron ore, gold, limestone, natural gas, silver and tungsten.

Road, rail, sea and air transport is good in New Zealand, and almost every family has a car. Geographically remote from other countries, New Zealand has good air and sea connections with the rest of the world.

New Zealand is a monarchy. It has the same queen, Elizabeth II, as Britain. In New Zealand, the Queen is represented by a governor-general. The government is headed by a prime minister. He and his cabinet are members of the elected House of Representatives, the nation's parliament.

The earliest-known people in New Zealand were Morioris—a Polynesian people. They were conquered in about the 1300's by another Polynesian people, Maoris, who settled mainly on the coastal parts of North Island.

Abel Tasman, commander of a ship sailing for the Dutch East India Company, sighted New Zealand in 1642. The Dutch named the islands after Zeeland, a province in the Netherlands. The Dutch kept their discovery secret. James Cook, a British sea captain, found and charted the island in 1769. But the British took little interest in the country for the next 70 years.

In 1839, Edward Gibbon Wakefield, a British statesman, who had formed a New Zealand Company, sent a group of British colonists to settle on the islands. The first colonists settled at Wellington. To protect them, the British government incorporated New Zealand into their Australian colony of New South Wales.

In 1840, Maori chiefs signed a treaty accepting British rule, and in 1841 New Zealand became a colony independent of Australia. Disputes about land led to war between the Maoris and the settlers in 1845-1846. Fighting occurred again between 1860 and 1870.

In 1907, New Zealand became an independent dominion within the British empire. Its troops fought in Europe in both World Wars. More recently New Zealand has sent troops into Vietnam to support the Australian and United States forces. These were withdrawn in 1972.

Niagara Falls are two waterfalls that occur in the Niagara River, on the borders of the United States and Canada. The Niagara River is a short river that connects Lake Erie with Lake Ontario. All the Great Lakes except for Lake Ontario empty into it. Goat Island divides the river just before the falls.

The falls themselves are set in beautiful scenery, and are a favourite resort for tourists, especially honeymooners. Half a million tons of water a minute fall into a steep gorge. The larger of the two streams falls on the Canadian side as the Horseshoe Falls. They are 158 feet high and 2,600 feet wide at their widest point. The American Falls are formed by the smaller stream. They are

Above: Niagara Falls. In the foreground is an observation tower overlooking the Horseshoe Falls.

Left: In 1859 Charles Blondin crossed Niagara on a tightrope. He subsequently repeated this feat carrying a man on his back.

167 feet high and about 1,000 feet wide. During the winter the falls sometimes freeze into a curtain of ice.

Many power plants have been installed near the falls to use their tremendous water power.

Nicaragua is a republic in Central America. It lies between Honduras and Costa Rica, and has coastlines on both the Atlantic and Pacific oceans. Along the Atlantic coast, there are forested low-

946

lands where the weather is hot and humid. Inland are highlands where the climate is cooler. The Pacific coast is low lying. Most of the people live there. In this region is the huge Lake Nicaragua. The country's area is 57,143 square miles.

Nicaragua's 1,984,000 inhabitants are mostly *mestizos* — that is, people of mixed European and American Indian descent. Spanish is the country's official language. Farming is the chief occupation. Export crops, such as cotton, coffee and sugarcane, grow well in the rich volcanic soil. Managua, the capital, was the leading manufacturing centre. In late 1972 it was almost destroyed by an earthquake.

A location map of Nicaragua.

The ruins of Managua after the earthquake that devastated the city in 1972.

A nickel concentrating plant in Kambalda, Australia.

Christopher Columbus reached Nicaragua in 1502. It became part of the Spanish colonies in America. In 1823, it joined a union of Central American countries. But in 1838 it became completely independent.

Nickel is used widely in the form of plating and in alloys. It is electroplated on metals such as steel to protect them from corrosion. (See Electroplating.) Nickel is added with chromium to steel to make it stainless. With copper, nickel forms a wide range of alloys, including the cupronickel used for 'silver' coinage and the nickel-silver used for cutlery. With chromium, nickel forms heat-resistant alloys which are used in jet engines and electric fires. Nickel is also used in nickel-iron and nickel-cadmium batteries. The main nickel ore is pentlandite.

Niger is a landlocked country in western Africa with an area of 489,190 square miles. Much of it lies within the Sahara and has dry and infertile land. But there are grasslands in the south, and the south-western corner is watered by the Niger River. In the south-east, part of Lake Chad lies within Niger's boundaries. Niamey, on the Niger River, is the capital city.

Niger has 3,800,000 people. About three-quarters of them belong to Hausa and

This map shows the location of Niger.

Djerma groups. They live in the south and are farmers, growing cotton, ground-nuts, millet, sorghum and rice. Farther north live nomadic Fulani and Tuareg groups, who move from place to place to find grazing for their cattle, goats and sheep. The groups speak different languages. Only a few people speak French, the official language of the country. The majority of people follow the Muslim religion.

Most of the people of Niger produce only enough food for their own needs. Some ground-nuts, meat and hides are exported, but lack of transport facilities hinders trade. Niger's most valuable mineral is uranium, mining of which is being developed under financial assistance from France.

Before Europeans came to Niger in the late 1700's, it was ruled by various groups, including Arabs and Berbers. Parts of what is now Niger belonged to the Ghana, Mali and Songhai empires. In the early 1900's France added the area to its colonial empire and made Niger a separate colony in 1922. Niger became a republic in the French Community in 1958. Two years later, it gained complete independence.

Nigeria, in western Africa, has the largest population of any African country. But 12 other African countries cover a larger area. The country is named after the long River Niger, which flows into the sea through a vast swampy delta.

The land varies from steaming-hot tropical forests and swamps in the south to grassland, merging into desert, in the north. In the south, the rainfall reaches more than 150 inches a year. In the far north, the average rainfall may be below 20 inches a year.

The four main groups of people are the Hausa and Fulani of the north, the Yoruba of the south-west, and the Ibo of the south-east. The Yoruba and Ibo are Negro people, but the Muslim Hausa and Fulani are Hamitic, a brown-skinned people with narrow noses and thin lips.

The cities of Nigeria are modern and most city-dwellers wear western dress. But many people wear colourful robes decorated with traditional patterns. In the villages, people still live in mud houses with thatched or corrugated iron roofs. About half the peole are Muslims, and about a quarter are Christians. The others follow tribal religions.

Farming is Nigeria's chief industry. Important crops include cocoa, ground-nuts (peanuts), palm kernels and palm oil. Tin and columbite are mined.

Left: A location map of Nigeria.

Below: A typical Nigerian market scene.

Facts and Figures
Area: 356,669 square miles.
Population: 55,100,000.
Capital: Lagos.

Nigeria was the home of several African civilizations, which produced some of the finest African art. British influence in Nigeria began in the 1700's. From 1906, Britain ruled the entire country.

Nigeria gained independence in 1960 and became a republic in 1963. In 1966, army officers overthrew the elected government. In 1967, the people of south-eastern Nigeria rebelled and established their own state of Biafra. The central government did not recognize Biafra and a terrible civil war began. It ended in 1970, by which time the people of Biafra were suffering from a famine. After the war was over, the International Red Cross and other charitable organizations airlifted food and other supplies to the region. The Nigerian leader, General Gowon, promised an amnesty to the rebels and called on the population to help rebuild the country.

Nightingale, Florence (1820-1910), completely changed people's attitude towards nursing in the 19th century. She organized care for wounded British soldiers in the Crimean War and was the first woman to give good hospital care to soldiers fighting outside their own country. Soldiers called Florence 'the lady with the lamp', because she walked through their hospital wards at night and the lamp's light was a symbol of her care.

Florence Nightingale was born near Florence, in Italy, where her wealthy parents were living. She spent most of her early life in England. She took an interest in helping other people, especially if they were ill. She studied nursing, and at 33 took charge of a London hospital.

The British became angry when they learnt that wounded British soldiers fighting in the Crimea had no proper care. Florence Nightingale went to Turkey to take charge of nursing the soldiers wounded in the Crimea. She left England with 38 nurses.

The problems Florence faced were enormous, but she proved to be a brilliant

Above: Scutari, where many of the British wounded from the Crimean War were taken, was a converted Turkish barracks. Florence Nightingale transformed it into an efficient hospital.

Left: A portrait of 'the Lady with the Lamp'.

organizer. She made sure the hospital was clean, and she made the government send supplies. She worked very hard, and nearly died from fever. But she recovered and stayed until the end of the war.

When she returned, she went quietly home and then moved to London to continue her nursing studies. The strain of overwork made her an invalid, but she continued her efforts to improve nursing care for the rest of her life.

Nile The Nile is a river of north-eastern Africa, and flows 4,160 miles from its source in the great lakes of central Africa to its wide delta on the Mediterranean. It is the longest river in the world. The largest of the Nile's tributaries is the Blue Nile, which rises in Ethiopia.

The Nile Valley and Delta, where the Nile widens out through channels to the Mediterranean, forms a long narrow oasis through the desert belt which stretches from Morocco to China. This fertile area

MEDITERRANEAN SEA

Alexandria

Cairo

Suez Canal

RED SEA

Egypt

Aswan Dam

Khartoum

Blue Nile

Sudan

White Nile

Lake Albert   Lake Kyoga

In its upper reaches the Nile has many tributaries, of which the largest is the Blue Nile.

Right: Spectacular waterfalls as the Blue Nile descends from the mountains of Ethiopia.

part of a scheme for irrigating over a thousand square miles of land in the province of Gezira.

Besides irrigation, the Nile is also used by trading boats to and from Cairo, which is situated at the head of the delta.

Alexandria, where Nelson fought the Battle of the Nile against the French Fleet in 1798, is situated at the west of the Delta. At the east of the Delta is Port Said, which is on the northern entrance of the Suez Canal.

Nitric acid (HNO_3) is an extremely corrosive acid, capable of dissolving most common metals. It does not dissolve gold. Even this will dissolve in *aqua regia*, a mixture of nitric and hydrochloric acids. In pure form, nitric acid is colourless, and has choking fumes. The acid has been a standard laboratory chemical since the alchemists used it in the Middle Ages. The chief of its many industrial uses are in making TNT and other explosives, nitrate fertilizers, dyes and drugs.

Nitrogen is a colourless, tasteless gas. It is a chemical element, symbol N. It is found in the air and the Earth's atmosphere is nearly four-fifths nitrogen. Chemically, nitrogen is inert—that is, it does not readily take part in chemical reactions. For instance, it does not burn, nor will it support combustion.

Nitrogen is essential to life in plants and animals. It is found in protoplasm (the material in cells) and in proteins,

is part of Egypt, and is highly cultivated and thickly populated. An area of over a million square miles is irrigated by the river and delta of the Nile. A series of huge dams controls the waters of the Nile, which flood down in spring and early summer from the mountains of Ethiopia. Two of the largest dams are those of the Gebel Awlia and Aswan reservoirs. The Gebel Awlia reservoir can hold 2,000 million cubic metres of water and the famous Aswan reservoir holds twice this amount.

There is also a great dam across the Blue Nile at the village of Makwar, near Sennar, in the Sudan. This was built as

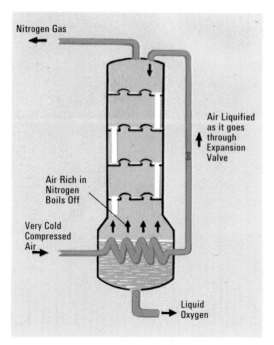

Nitrogen Gas

Air Liquified as it goes through Expansion Valve

Air Rich in Nitrogen Boils Off

Very Cold Compressed Air

Liquid Oxygen

A simplified rectification column for separating oxygen and nitrogen. When liquid air comes into contact with cool gaseous air, nitrogen gas tends to boil off, while oxygen collects in the liquid. Almost pure nitrogen gas can be taken from the top of the column, while liquid oxygen can be removed from the base.

Right: Nitrogen encourages rapid plant growth. It is taken in through the roots mainly as nitrate dissolved in the soil water. The plant on the left has been starved of nitrogen.

Nkrumah, Kwame (1909-1972) became the first political leader of Ghana after the country gained independence in 1957. He had campaigned for many years for an end to British colonial rule in the Gold Coast, as Ghana had previously been named.

Nkrumah was born in the Gold Coast. He was educated in the United States

Kwame Nkrumah, Ghanaian leader exiled for corruption.

which consist mainly of nitrogen-containing compounds called amino-acids. Plants get their nitrogen from compounds in the soil. These, in turn, get their nitrogen from the air or from fertilizers and decaying matter. Animals get their nitrogen by eating plants or by eating other animals. The way in which nitrogen passes from the soil to plants and animals and then back to the soil again is an important part of the balance of nature called the *nitrogen cycle*.

Animals also breathe in nitrogen. But it is not absorbed by the lungs and is breathed out again. Nitrogen is extracted from air for industrial use by cooling the air until it liquifies. The liquid air so formed is separated into its components, oxygen and nitrogen. Nitrogen also occurs in mineral deposits of nitrates in South America and Europe. It is used for making ammonia, fertilizers, explosives and plastics. Other nitrogen compounds are used as drugs.

951

and England. He was prime minister of the colony at the time the new nation of Ghana was born. He kept that post in the new government. In 1960 Ghana became a republic, and Nkrumah became its president.

Nkrumah symbolized the national pride of the Ghanaian people. He sought to make Africa politically stronger by encouraging African nations to work together. But before long he began to rule his country as a dictator. He destroyed political parties other than his own. He jailed his opponents. His government was accused of corruption, and the economy of Ghana nearly collapsed. In 1966, the army seized control while Nkrumah was visiting China. He was given refuge in Guinea, where he was made honorary co-president of the country.

Nobel, Alfred Bernhard (1833-1896), was a Swedish chemist and inventor. He is most famous for the discovery of dynamite and for establishing the annual Nobel prizes.

Nobel's father was a manufacturer of nitroglycerine. Many accidents took place during the handling of this highly dangerous explosive, and Nobel was determined to find a way of making it safe. Eventually, by mixing the nitroglycerine with an absorbent substance called *Kieselguhr*, Nobel made a manageable explosive which he called *dynamite*. He also invented a blasting jelly and a smokeless gunpowder. Soon his factories sprang up all over the world.

Alfred Nobel aged thirty. He became one of the richest men of his day, but died a lonely and unhappy man.

But the knowledge that his inventions were being used for such violent acts as killing and destruction, rather than the peaceful purposes he had hoped for, weighed heavily on Nobel's conscience. In his will, Nobel set aside a large sum of money to be used for awarding annual prizes for outstanding achievements in several different spheres. Nobel chose the fields of chemistry, physics, medicine or physiology, literature, and the advancement of peace. These prizes are highly esteemed as well as being financially valuable, and were first awarded in 1901.

Nobel prizes are awarded annually to people or institutions whose work is considered to have benefited mankind. The prizes come from a fund of over £3 million established in the will of the Swedish inventor Alfred Nobel. Each year, the income from the fund is divided into five equal parts to provide one prize in each of the following fields: physics; chemistry; physiology and medicine; literature; and work for international peace. In 1969, the Swedish Central Bank established a fund for an additional prize in economics.

The Royal Academy of Science in Stockholm selects the prizewinners in physics, chemistry and economics. The Caroline Institute in Stockholm decides the award of the prize for medicine and physiology, and the Swedish Academy of Literature the prize for literature. A five-man committee selected by the Norwegian parliament chooses the recipient of the peace prize.

The ceremonies of awarding the prizes takes place each December 10th, the anniversary of Nobel's death. The peace prize is given in Oslo, the others in Stockholm. In any particular year, awards

Linus Pauling, an American scientist, is the only person to have won two individual Nobel prizes. In 1954 he won the chemistry prize for his discoveries about molecules. He won the peace prize in 1963 for his protests against nuclear bomb tests.

FAMOUS NOBEL PRIZEWINNERS

Physics

1901	Wilhelm Roentgen	Germany
1903	Antoine Henri Becquerel	France
	Pierre Curie	France
	Marie Curie	France
1909	Guglielmo Marconi	Italy
	Karl Braun	Germany
1918	Max Planck	Germany
1921	Albert Einstein	Switzerland
1922	Niels Bohr	Denmark
1938	Enrico Fermi	Italy
1939	Ernest O. Lawrence	USA

Chemistry

1908	Ernest Rutherford	Britain
1911	Marie Curie	France
1934	Harold Urey	USA
1935	Frédéric Joliot	France
	Irène Joliot-Curie	France
1951	Glenn Seaborg	USA
	Edwin McMillan	USA
1954	Linus Pauling	USA

Physiology and Medicine

1904	Ivan Pavlov	Russia
1905	Robert Koch	Germany
1908	Paul Ehrlich	Germany
	Elie Metchnikoff	Russia
1923	Sir Frederick Banting	Canada
	John J. R. Macleod	Britain
1945	Sir Alexander Fleming	Britain
	Sir Howard Florey	Britain
	Ernst Chain	Britain
1952	Selman Waksman	USA

1962	James Watson	USA
	Francis Crick	Britain
	Maurice Wilkins	Britain

Literature

1907	Rudyard Kipling	Britain
1913	Sir Rabindranath Tagore	India
1920	Knut Hamsun	Norway
1921	Anatole France	France
1923	William Butler Yeats	Ireland
1925	George Bernard Shaw	Britain
1929	Thomas Mann	Germany
1932	John Galsworthy	Britain
1946	Herman Hesse	Germany
1948	T. S. Eliot	Britain
1949	William Faulkner	USA
1950	Bertrand Russell	Britain
1953	Sir Winston Churchill	Britain
1954	Ernest Hemingway	USA
1957	Albert Camus	France
1958	Boris Pasternak	USSR
1971	Pablo Neruda	Chile
1973	Patrick White	Australia

Peace

1917	International Red Cross	
1919	Woodrow Wilson	USA
1925	Sir Austen Chamberlain	Britain
	Charles Dawes	USA
1944	International Red Cross	
1952	Albert Schweitzer	France
1953	George C. Marshall	USA
1957	Lester Pearson	Canada
1961	Dag Hammarskjöld	Sweden
1962	Linus Pauling	USA
1964	Martin Luther King, Jr.	USA
1965	UNICEF	
1971	Willy Brandt	Germany

are made only if the judges consider the candidates worthy. The first award was made in 1901.

Noise When we talk about *noise* we generally mean sounds that are unpleasant or that interfere with our comfort. Almost everyone finds loud, shrill or crashing sounds objectionable, but even pleasant sounds can cause discomfort in some circumstances. For example, music or low conversation can be annoying to someone who is trying to sleep.

Discordant noises differ from pure, musical tones in the fact that their vibrations are random and irregular. Usually, as with the common noise of dustbins being emptied, unpleasant sounds are also fairly high in their range of pitch. If every pitch were represented in the sound the result would be a bland, hissing sound called *white noise*.

Excessively loud noise—above 130 decibels or so on the sound scale—can cause pain. Continuous exposure to sounds of 85 decibels or more can cause permanent damage to the hearing. Such levels are commonly found in noisy offices, factories, busy traffic areas and discotheques. But even when noise does not hurt us physically, it may have damaging psychological effects. It can make us irritable or tense and can lower our efficiency for work. People are becoming increasingly aware of the dangers of 'noise pollution' in modern life. Experts urge the need for laws to curb car, aircraft and machine noises.

In electronics, the term *noise* refers

to any interference in a signal being transmitted. This may be sound in the case of radio or telephone signals, but can be visual interference in the case of television or radar signals.

Talking points
* Modern technology — aircraft, cars, machinery — has made the world much noisier than it has ever been. Discuss how it could be made quieter again, without causing serious inconvenience.
* Discuss why some noises, such as music, are pleasant to listen to, while others, such as the squeal of brakes, can be unpleasant.
* Almost everywhere you can hear *some* noise — distant traffic, birds singing, wind or the sea. You may not notice it because your ears only hear the sounds they listen to, unless the sounds are very loud. Can you think of any situation where there would be perfect silence?

Articles to read
Acoustics; Loudspeaker, Microphone; Music; Radio; Sonar; Sound; Supersonic flight; Television; Ultrasonics; Voice.

Nomads are people who wander from place to place and have no permanent home. They usually travel within certain general areas according to the seasons and the supply of food. Hunting nomads, such as the pygmies of Africa and Asia, follow the animals that they kill to eat. Pastoral nomads, such as the Bedouins of North Africa, drive their herds of camels, goats, sheep and horses from one patch of grazing land to another. There is not enough vegetation to set up permanent farms.

Nomads generally live in tents or some equally simple type of shelter, and carry few belongings with them.

Norfolk (area 2,053 square miles), a maritime county of eastern England, forms part of the district known as East Anglia. Its county town and only industrial centre is Norwich, and its population is 616,500.

Norfolk is almost all flat and low-lying, apart from cliffs at Cromer on the North Sea coast. The soil is fertile, composed mainly of chalk, sand and loam. The county is drained by the Bure, Great Ouse, Waveney and Yare rivers. There are *fens* (low, marshy land sometimes covered with water) in the west of

Turkish nomads travel around in search of grazings for their flocks of sheep. Donkeys carry the black tents in which they live.

Norfolk is renowned for
the lakes and waterways
called The Broads
where many holiday-
makers hire sailing boats
and motor cruisers.

Norfolk is renowned for the lakes and waterways called The Broads where many holiday-makers hire sailing boats and motor cruisers.

the county and huge mudbanks in the region of The Wash, a large bay in the north-west. The sea has also made inroads on parts of the coast. The series of lakes and waterways called The Broads is rich in plant and wild life and attracts thousands of boating and fishing enthusiasts every year.

Wheat, barley, sugar-beet and turnips are grown and turkeys and geese are reared for the London market. Fishing is centred on Yarmouth and Lowestoft.

Norfolk Island, a picturesque island in the Pacific Ocean, is a popular tourist resort for Australians and New Zealanders. It is about 900 miles north-east of Sydney and about 500 miles north-west of New Zealand's North Island. Together with two small uninhabited islands it forms an Australian territory. An administrator appointed by the Australian government has his office at Kingston.

Norfolk Island has an area of about 14 square miles. Its coasts are steep and have no harbours. Visitors travel by air from Sydney or Auckland, or are ferried ashore from ships in surf-boats. The island is hilly and has rich vegetation, including fruit trees and magnificent pines. It has facilities for swimming, boating, hiking and other sports. The weather is warm all year round.

The resident population of the island is 1,240. Many inhabitants are retired people. Others work in hotels and shops that serve the needs of visitors. The island exports some fruit and fish. Formerly, it had a whaling industry.

Captain James Cook claimed the island for Britain when he arrived there in 1774. It was used as a penal settlement from 1788 to 1813 and again from 1825 to 1856.

Norse myths The early Scandinavian peoples, who lived in the countries now called Sweden, Denmark, Norway and Iceland, invented a series of tales about the formation of the Earth and the activities of the gods and goddesses they believed in. These tales, which make up the Norse mythology, are contained in large collections, known as the *Eddas*.

According to the *Eddas,* before the Earth was formed, there were only two vague divisions of the Universe—a world of mist and a world of light. Fountains in the world of mist froze into ice. Warm winds from the other world melted some of the ice to vapour. From this vapour, so the story goes, sprang the giant Ymir and his children. Later, a god was created. He married a giant and they had three children: Odin, Vili and Ve. The legends relate how these three killed Ymir and created from his body the homes of the gods, the giants, and man, and a region of darkness where the dead who had not died in battle were forced to dwell.

Odin became chief among the gods, and was said to inhabit a magnificent palace, Valhalla. There he sat with two ravens perched on his shoulders.

The Norsemen had a demon god, called Loki. Many stories tell of his treachery. Balder, son of Odin, was handsome, wise and popular. His mother, Frigg, made all living and non-living things swear never to harm Balder. But Loki found out that Frigg had forgotten to ask one plant—the mistletoe—to spare Balder. He tricked Hod, the blind god of night, into killing Balder by throwing a piece of mistletoe at him.

The death of Balder was the beginning of the end. Loki led the giants and demons in a gigantic war against the gods. One by one the gods perished, even Odin and Thor. The end of the gods brought the doom of mankind. Earth, sky, stars and all things collapsed into the dark nothingness from which everything had come.

Thor was the Norse god of thunder. He was a mighty warrior and fought with and killed many giants and monsters. He was armed with a hammer called Mjolnir (destroyer). He would throw this at his enemies and it never failed to strike them down.

North America is the third largest of the world's continents and occupies nearly a fifth of the Earth's land area. Only Asia and Africa are larger. Its physical limits are Panama in the south, and Alaska and Greenland in the north. The northern four-fifths of the continent are occupied by Canada and the United States, while the remainder is made up of Mexico and Central America. There are also a large number of islands, the most important of which are the Caribbean Islands and Greenland, the world's largest.

North America has an area of 9,635,000 square miles. It is almost as wide as it is long: from north to south it stretches some 4,500 miles, and from east to west about 4,000 miles. It has a population of about 300,000,000.

Its land regions are fairly ,well marked. The Lawrentian region is an area of low-lying rocky land that stretches round Hudson Bay. It extends from the Arctic Ocean in the north to Labrador in the east. Much of it is unexplored forest, well watered with icy lakes and streams.

The Appalachian region consists of a range of mountains running south-west-wards from Quebec in Canada to Alabama in the south-eastern United States. The Appalachians include the Allegheny plateau and other mountain ranges.

In the south of the continent, bordering the Gulf of Mexico and the Atlantic Ocean, there are flat coastal plains. Vast areas of these plains are swampy.

To the west lie the great Western Highlands. They are called the Cordilleras in Central America, and the Rocky Mountains in the rest of the continent. They stretch from Alaska to Central America. The highest peak in North America is Mt McKinley (20,320 ft), in Alaska, but in the Colorado Rockies alone there are 55 peaks that reach 14,000 feet or more. Running parallel to the Rockies are the Coast and Cascade ranges, and the Sierra Nevada. They border a narrow, fertile, coastal strip along the shores of the Pacific.

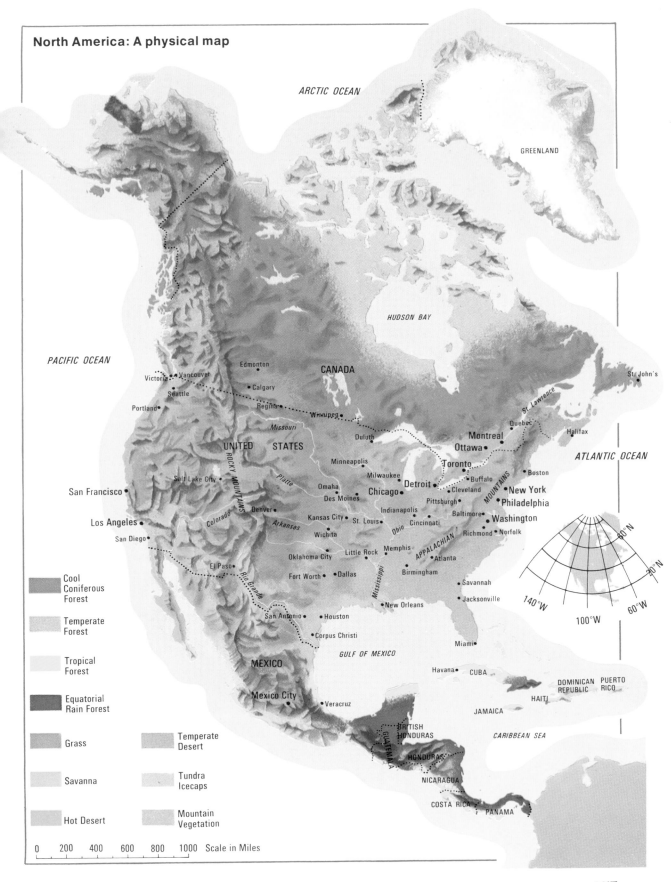

North America: A physical map

ARCTIC OCEAN

GREENLAND

PACIFIC OCEAN

HUDSON BAY

St. John's

Edmonton
CANADA
Victoria • Vancouver
Calgary
Seattle
Portland
Regina
Winnipeg
Missouri
St. Lawrence
Quebec
Halifax
Duluth
Montreal
Ottawa
ATLANTIC OCEAN
UNITED   STATES
Minneapolis
Toronto
Milwaukee
Buffalo
Boston
Salt Lake City
Omaha
Des Moines
Chicago
Detroit
Cleveland
New York
San Francisco
Denver
Platte
Kansas City
St. Louis
Indianapolis
Pittsburgh
Baltimore
Philadelphia
Los Angeles
Colorado
Arkansas
Wichita
Ohio
Cincinnati
Washington
Richmond
Norfolk
San Diego
Oklahoma City
Little Rock
Memphis
APPALACHIAN
El Paso
Fort Worth
Dallas
Birmingham
Atlanta
Rio Grande
Mississippi
Savannah
San Antonio
Houston
New Orleans
Jacksonville
Corpus Christi
Miami
GULF OF MEXICO
MEXICO
Havana
CUBA
DOMINICAN
REPUBLIC
PUERTO
RICO
Mexico City
HAITI
Veracruz
JAMAICA
CARIBBEAN SEA
BRITISH
HONDURAS
GUATEMALA
HONDURAS
NICARAGUA
COSTA RICA
PANAMA

ROCKY MOUNTAINS
MOUNTAINS

60°N
40°N
20°N
140°W
100°W
60°W

Legend

- Cool Coniferous Forest
- Temperate Forest
- Tropical Forest
- Equatorial Rain Forest
- Grass
- Savanna
- Hot Desert
- Temperate Desert
- Tundra Icecaps
- Mountain Vegetation

0 200 400 600 800 1000   Scale in Miles

957

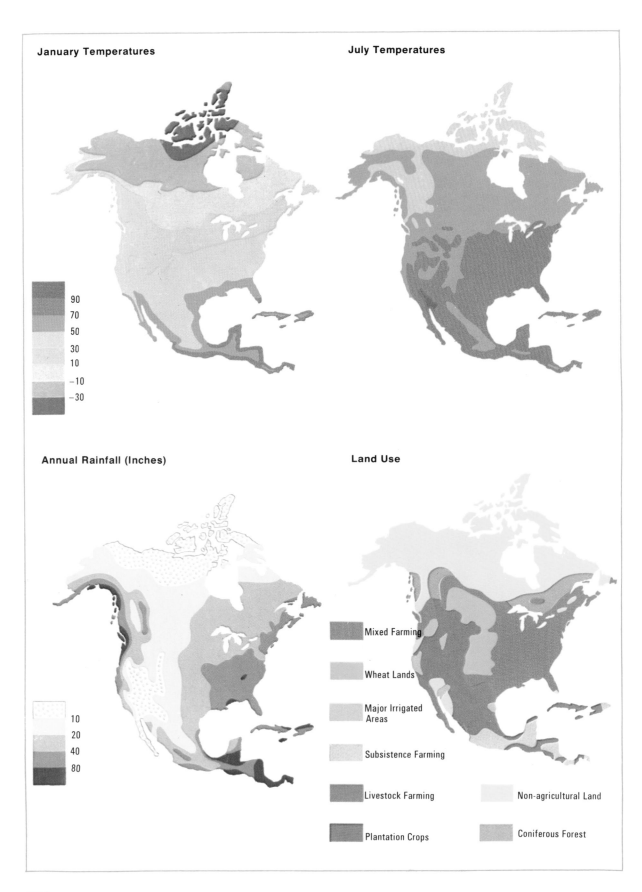

January Temperatures

July Temperatures

90
70
50
30
10
−10
−30

Annual Rainfall (Inches)

10
20
40
80

Land Use

Mixed Farming

Wheat Lands

Major Irrigated Areas

Subsistence Farming

Livestock Farming

Plantation Crops

Non-agricultural Land

Coniferous Forest

The Great Plains form a 1,500-mile-wide belt, including part of central and northern Canada and the interior of the United States. These are great grazing and grain-growing lands.

Rivers flow westwards to the west of the Rockies, and eastwards, southwards, and northwards on the eastern side of the mountains. Westward-flowing rivers, such as the Yukon, Snake, and Colorado are generally swift torrents. The Missouri-Mississippi river system is 3,700 miles long, one of the longest in the world. The St. Lawrence flows eastwards and connects the Great Lakes with the Atlantic.

The Great Lakes, on the borders of Canada and the United States, are the most important in the world. They are lakes Superior, Michigan, Huron, Erie and Ontario. The best known falls are the Niagara Falls, which are famed for their striking scenery.

The climate in the far south is always warm, and in the far north it is always cold. Most of the continent has warm summers and cold winters. Rainfall is heavy (up to 140 inches a year) on the western slopes of the Rockies; but in the desert regions there may be only about 1½ inches of rain a year.

North America is still very rich in animal life, but as the population increases and spreads, the wildlife is rapidly disappearing from the continent. A hundred years ago the plains were filled with enormous herds of bison. Today, only a few herds remain, carefully protected in

A map showing the distribution of population in North America.

COUNTRIES OF NORTH AMERICA

Country	Area (sq. mi.)	Population	Capital
Canada	3,851,809	21,324,000	Ottawa
Costa Rica	19,575	1,800,000	San José
Cuba	44,178	8,553,000	Havana
Dominican Republic	18,816	4,021,000	Santo Domingo
El Salvador	8,260	3,390,000	San Salvador
Guatemala	42,042	5,014,000	Guatemala
Haiti	10,714	4,768,000	Port-au-Prince
Honduras	43,277	2,535,000	Tegucigalpa
Jamaica	4,232	1,861,000	Kingston
Mexico	761,602	48,313,000	Mexico City
Nicaragua	57,143	1,984,000	Managua
Panama	29,209	1,428,000	Panama
Trinidad and Tobago	1,980	1,010,000	Port-of-Spain
United States (excluding Hawaii)	3,669,209	203,166,000	Washington D.C.

TERRITORIES OF NORTH AMERICA

Territory	Area (sq. mi.)	Population	Capital	Status
Bahamas	4,400	169,000	Nassau	British colony
Bermuda	21	51,000	Hamilton	British colony
Greenland	840,001	50,000	Godthaab	County of Denmark
Guadeloupe	687	323,000	Point à Pitre	Overseas department of France
Honduras, British	8,867	122,000	Belize	British colony
Martinique	425	332,000	Fort-de-France	Overseas department of France
Netherlands Antilles	371	224,000	Willemstad	Self-governing member of the Kingdom of The Netherlands
Panama Canal Zone	647	51,000	Balboa Heights	U.S. leasehold from Panama
Puerto Rico	3,435	2,712,000	San Juan	U.S. commonwealth
Saint Pierre and Miquelon	93	5,000	Saint Pierre	French overseas territory
Virgin Islands (British)	59	10,000	Road Town	British colony
Virgin Islands (U.S.)	132	62,000	Charlotte Amalie	U.S. territory

game preserves. Nevertheless, the woods of central and eastern North America still hold black bears, deer, musquash, porcupines and beavers. The Rockies are the home of eagles, grizzly bears, elk, and moose. In the far north are found some of the most valuable fur-bearing animals, including Arctic foxes, fur seals and polar bears. Tropical creatures such as alligators, monkeys, jaguars, ant-eaters, armadillos and a host of colourful birds inhabit Central America.

North America's plant life varies from the mosses and lichens that survive in the coldest regions of the Arctic, to the desert cactus of the waterless areas of the south-west. Trees include the red-woods and sequoias of California, the largest trees in the world, maples (whose leaf is the emblem of Canada) and tropical palms. Canada has enormous forests of fir, spruce and pine. The vast grasslands of the Great Plains feed herds of sheep and cattle.

North American agriculture is strikingly uneven. In the United States and Canada there are millions of acres of fertile land, and the yield per acre is constantly increasing because farmers use the latest equipment and methods. Canada exports more than half its wheat harvest to other countries. But in the Latin American countries of the continent the land is so poor and farming methods and machinery so out-of-date that there is barely enough food produced to feed the population. Coffee, bananas and sugar are the chief crops of most of the Central American countries.

North America has some of the world's richest deposits of minerals. The most important are coal, petroleum, gold, iron, nickel, silver, lead, zinc and copper. Both Canada and the United States are

among the leading industrial nations of the world, with large manufacturing centres in many places. But the Latin American countries import a large quantity of their manufactured goods, because local industries cannot supply all the country's needs.

Most of the people in the Latin American countries of the continent speak Spanish, but in the United States and Canada, English (with some French in Canada) is the main language.

Some of the world's greatest cities are located in North America. The largest Canadian cities are Montreal, Toronto and Vancouver. In the United States, New York City, Los Angeles, Chicago, Philadelphia, Detroit and Houston are the main population centres, each with more than a million people. In the Latin American countries Mexico City and Havana, in Cuba, are the largest cities.

The first European explorers reached North America nearly 500 years ago. The wild region they found was inhabited by Indians who are believed to have come originally from Asia. They have certain similarities to the Mongols. The Aztec and Maya Indians of Mexico had developed a high standard of civilization, but the northern Indians lived in primitive conditions.

In the far north the Eskimos arrived from Asia about 2,000 years ago. Most inhabitants of the continent have European ancestors, but about a tenth of the people are Negroes, originally brought from Africa as slaves.

Northamptonshire (area 914 square miles), a county in the east Midlands of England, has a reputation for its many beautiful church spires. It is also one of the traditional fox-hunting counties. Its county town is Northampton, and its population is 468,000.

The generally rolling land is drained by the River Nene and its tributaries into the Wash. Iron ore is mined, particularly in the region of Kettering, Welling-

North America has extremes of climate. A temperature of 134°F has been recorded in Death Valley, California. In contrast −74°F has occurred on Ellesmere Island, Canada. Death Valley receives a yearly average rainfall of about 1½ inches. Parts of Washington state have over 140 inches per year.

borough and Corby. Metal manufacturing is a major industry in Northampton and Corby. The other great industry is boot and shoe making. Food processing, tanning and the manufacture of clothing and leather goods are also important. Beef and dairy cattle graze on the lush pastureland and the fertile clay soil produces good crops of sugar-beet, wheat and barley.

North Carolina is a Southern state on the Atlantic coast of the United States. It was one of the 13 original British colonies. Of the 5,082,000 people who live there,

Contrasting North American landscapes

Above right: Not all of Alaska is a frozen waste. In some places quick-growing crops can be produced during the short summers.
Right: The Potomac River divides Virginia from Maryland, and flows out into Chesapeake Bay.
Below: Elephant Rock in the Valley of Fire State Park, Nevada. Much of the southern and central part of North America is desert or semi-arid country. In these areas the forces of erosion sometimes carve rock into fantastic shapes.

The legislative building or State House of North Carolina. It was the first building in any state erected for the sole use of the legislature and was opened in 1963.

more than half live in rural areas. The state capital is Raleigh, and the largest city is Charlotte.

North Carolina has three natural regions: the Blue Ridge Mountains in the west, the Piedmont Plateau in the centre and the coastal plain in the east. Although farming is important, North Carolina is also the leading manufacturing state of the South. It produces about two-fifths of all the tobacco grown in the United States. Much cotton is grown also. Factories process the tobacco, and produce textiles—not only cotton but also woollen and synthetic fabrics. The prosperous furniture industry uses wood from the forests that cover more than half the state.

Sir Walter Raleigh, the famous adventurer, sent a party of men and women to Roanoke Island off the coast of North Carolina in 1585. This settlement lasted only a year, but was the first English colony in North America. In 1587, another colony was founded there, but it had disappeared without a trace by 1590. It became known as the 'Lost Colony'.

North Dakota is a state in the midwestern region of the United States. Its countryside includes fertile river valleys, many lakes, rolling plains and the region of rugged cliffs and strange rock formations in the southwest known as the *Badlands*. The state has an area of more than 70,500 square miles, but has fewer than 618,000 people. Though most inhabitants still live in rural areas, the towns are of growing importance. Bismarck is the capital, but Fargo is the largest city.

North Dakota's income comes mainly from agriculture. Many of the people who

This map shows the location of North Carolina.

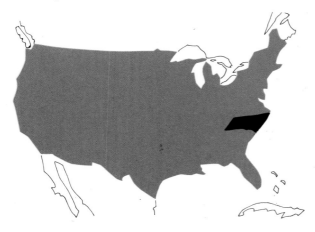

962

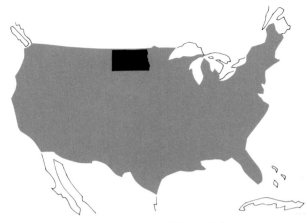

This map shows the location of North Dakota.

United States acquired part of the land from France in 1803 and the rest from Britain in 1818. The Dakota Territory was formed in 1861, and in 1889 North Dakota and South Dakota became separate states.

Northern Territory is a generally flat, rocky and undeveloped region in north-central Australia. About four-fifths of it is in the tropics, and much of its centre and south is desert. It has hills in some places; peaks of the Macdonnell Ranges in the south rise to over 4,000 feet. The territory has an area of 520,280 square miles, but only 74,000 people live there. Roughly one-third of the inhabitants are Aborigines, many of whom live on reserves set aside for them by the government. The chief town of the Territory is Darwin, a port which can handle large ships.

settled in the state in the late 1800's established wheat farms, and wheat is still the chief crop today. Ranchers raise beef and dairy cattle, pigs and sheep. North Dakota's valuable minerals include oil, natural gas and lignite coal. Manufacturing is limited mainly to the processing of farm produce.

Many Indian tribes lived in North Dakota before Europeans came. The

An unfavourable climate and problems of water supply have hindered development of the Northern Territory. Except

Near Brunnette Downs in Australia's Northern Territory. This region generally has little rain and many areas are subject to periods of drought. Cattle raising is one of the chief industries.

This location map shows Northern Territory.

in the north, many regions are too dry for growing crops. The chief source of irrigation is underground water from artesian wells, and these can be bored only in some parts. In the north, where rivers flow all the year round and monsoon rains fall from December to March, vegetation grows well, but flooding sometimes causes difficulties for farmers in this region.

Development is also limited by lack of transport. Railway lines run only in the northwest between Darwin and Birdum, and in the south from Alice Springs to South Australia. The total length of track is only some 500 miles. Livestock and produce for export must reach the rail terminals by lorry over the few highways or so-called 'beef roads'. Air transport is important, and serves not only Darwin but many small towns and settlements. Many of the territory's inland stations rely on radio to link them with medical and other help. (See Flying Doctor Service.)

The raising of beef cattle is a major industry. Large herds of cattle graze on huge inland stations. Horses and sheep are bred as well, though not in large numbers. Mining is a leading source of income. Gold, silver and copper are mined in the interior at Tennant Creek. In Arnhem Land, in the north, large deposits of bauxite are found, and since 1949 uranium has been produced near Rum Jungle in the north-west. The tourist trade centres around Alice Springs.

The mountains of the Macdonnell Ranges, with their spectacular chasms, draw visitors from far away.

Dutch sailors from Java were the first Europeans to reach the northern coast of the Territory, in the 1600's. Settlement was begun by the British over 200 years later, in the 1820's, but early efforts were hampered by disease and opposition from the Aborigines. Britain made South Australia responsible for the Territory in 1863, and tried to encourage settlement through land grants. Mining brought some settlers, and improved communications helped also. After the formation of the Commonwealth, the Territory came under federal control in 1911. From 1927 it was divided into two sections, but was reunited in 1931. It is administered from Darwin by an Administrator appointed by the federal government. A Legislative Council makes ordinances for the Territory, but these must be approved by the federal government.

North Pole This is the northern end of the Earth's axis, situated some 450 miles north of Greenland in the ice-strewn Arctic Ocean.

As long ago as 1893, Fridtjof Nansen, a Danish explorer, tried to reach the North Pole but came only within 260 miles of it. The Pole was eventually reached in 1909 by Robert E. Peary, an American

An exploration party at the North Pole.

The fishing harbour of Whitby, in Yorkshire, from which for centuries fishermen sailed to the North Sea to gain their living.

from the civil engineering branch of the U.S. Navy. The Peary Arctic Club was formed in New York to finance his expeditions. Flights were made over the polar ice in 1926, and, eventually, in 1930, a young Englishman, Gino Watkins, investigated the possibility of permanent air routes. There are now regularly scheduled flights passing close to, or over, the North Pole.

North Sea separates the island of Great Britain from the mainland of Europe. It is an extension of the Atlantic Ocean. Scientists believe that what is now the North Sea was once dry land. It consisted of wooded plains, on which many kinds of animals lived. The area was flooded about 8,000 years ago when the level of the Atlantic rose.

The North Sea extends about 600 miles in a north-south direction, from the Shetland Islands to Belgium. It is about 360 miles wide at the widest part. Its area is about 220,000 square miles. In the south, the Straits of Dover connect the North Sea with the English Channel. To the north of Denmark, two channels called the Skagerrak and the Kattegat link it with the Baltic Sea. The Kiel Canal also links the North Sea and the Baltic.

The North Sea is generally shallow — about 300 feet deep. However, near the Norwegian coast it reaches a depth of 2,400 feet. Some of Europe's chief rivers flow into the North Sea. Because of the amount of river water it receives, it is less salty than the Atlantic.

The countries that border on the North Sea are Britain, Belgium, the Netherlands, Germany, Denmark and Norway. All these countries have North Sea ports. Among the biggest are Hamburg, Antwerp and Rotterdam.

The North Sea provides the countries that surround it with valuable products. About 1,600,000 tons of fish are caught in its waters every year. Herring is the most abundant catch. Other fishes are cod, haddock, whiting and plaice. Many of the fish are caught in shallow *banks*. The Dogger Bank, between England and Denmark, is only 56 feet deep.

Natural gas was discovered under the North Sea in the 1950's. Since then, Britain, Norway and the Netherlands have built drilling rigs to bring the gas up. It is piped or shipped to the mainland. In the 1970's valuable deposits of oil have been found off the Scottish coast.

Northumberland (area 2,020 square miles) is England's most northerly county. Its county town is Newcastle-upon-Tyne, and its population is 795,000.

Flat in the east, the land rises to the Pennine Hills in the west and the Cheviot Hills in the north-west. The Tyne, Blyth and Coquet are the chief rivers. Rough grazing and permanent grass encourage sheep-rearing, but there is also considerable mixed and dairy farming.

The huge manufacturing region of Tyneside, developed from the Northumberland coalfield, includes coalmines, shipbuilding and engineering works, chemical works and allied industries. The main towns are Newcastle, Tynemouth, Wallsend, Blyth, Whitley Bay and Berwick-on-Tweed.

A savage history of war against the Scots has left a rich legacy of medieval castles and the remains of Hadrian's Wall.

North-west Passage is a sea route around the north of North America, connecting the Atlantic and Pacific oceans. The route leads from the Atlantic through either Baffin Bay or the Hudson Strait. It then continues between the Canadian Arctic islands, and through the Arctic Ocean and the Bering Strait. Finally it reaches the Bering Sea and the Pacific Ocean.

Beginning in the 1500's European trading companies, such as the Hudson's Bay Company, financed expeditions in search of the North-west Passage. They hoped to find a quick route from Europe for the profitable spice trade of the East Indies. The search for the passage continued for hundreds of years.

Among the early explorers who looked for the passage were the Englishmen William Baffin and Henry Hudson. Later, Sir John Franklin nearly completed the route. In 1906, the Norwegian explorer Roald Amundsen finally became the first to sail the North-west Passage.

Northwest Territories is a vast wild region of northern Canada. It has about one-third of the total land area of the country, but has only 33,000 inhabitants. Many of its people are Eskimos or American Indians.

The Northwest Territories borders on the provinces of Manitoba, Saskatchewan, Alberta and British Columbia in the south. To the west lies the Yukon. The total area of the Northwest Territories is 1,304,903 square miles. It is divided into three districts.

The *District of Franklin,* in the north and north-east, consists chiefly of numerous islands. The largest are Victoria, Ellesmere and Baffin islands. This district lies within the Arctic Circle. Its winters are bitter. Even in summer the ground remains permanently frozen. No trees and few other plants of any kind can survive. Eskimos live in the district. There are a few weather stations.

The *District of Keewatin* consists of

A location map of the Northwest Territories.

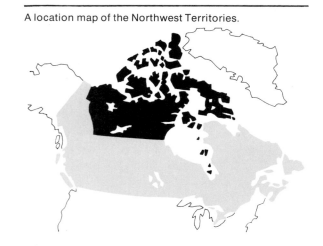

land west of Hudson Bay, and islands in Hudson Bay and James Bay. It is a bleak and cold region. Eskimos inhabit the shore of Hudson Bay.

The *District of Mackenzie* in the west is the most densely populated district. Most of the Indians and white people live there. The district includes the Mackenzie Mountains, with peaks rising more than 9,000 feet. Two huge inland bodies of water—the Great Slave Lake and Great Bear Lake—lie within the district. Canada's longest river, the Mackenzie, flows through it to the Arctic Ocean. This district has a number of towns and settlements. Yellowknife, the largest town in the Territories, is the territorial capital.

Mining is the leading industry in the Northwest Territories. Gold is produced at Yellowknife. Elsewhere, oil, zinc and lead are produced. Other minerals such as natural gas and iron remain to be fully exploited. Many of the Indians and Eskimos obtain their food by fishing and hunting. White fish and trout are caught in the Great Slave Lake and in coastal waters. The fur-bearing animals that are trapped include mink, muskrat and Arctic white fox.

Norway is a long, narrow country forming the extreme north-west part of the mainland of Europe. With Sweden, it forms the Scandinavian peninsula. Its west coast faces the North Sea and its northern coast the Barents Sea. The northern third of the country lies north of the Arctic Circle.

The western and northern parts of Norway consist of a high mountain range, sloping steeply to the sea. The coastline is jagged, with many offshore islands and *fiords*—deep sea inlets forming good all-weather harbours. Short, swift streams flow down the mountains.

In the south are broad high plateaux, many of them covered with snow and glaciers. Fertile lowlands lie in the south-east, where the capital, Oslo, is located.

About a quarter of the land is forested but nearly three-quarters is barren and unproductive. Only about one-thirtieth of the land can be cultivated, though some

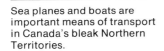

Sea planes and boats are important means of transport in Canada's bleak Northern Territories.

of the high valleys provide good summer pasture. The cattle grazing there are taken to lower ground in the winter.

The warm Gulf Stream flows northwards off the coast of Norway. As a result, Norway's coast has a mild climate, with warm summers and temperatures only just below freezing in the winter. The rainfall is heavy, reaching more than 200 inches a year in some mountain areas, but as little as 30 inches in the east.

The summer days are long, and in the far north there is continuous daylight for two months of the year.

Most Norwegians are descendants of the ancient Vikings. Many have fair hair and blue eyes. In the north, in an area called *Lapland* that extends across Norway, Sweden, Finland and into Russia, about 20,000 Lapps live. Many Lapps are *nomads* or wanderers who herd reindeer.

Fishing is a major industry in Norway. Norway is also the world's leading whaling country. Dairy farming and animal rearing are important types of farming. Mining and manufacturing is also important. Norway has deposits of several minerals, including bauxite, copper, iron and titanium ores. The swift rivers provide hydro-electric power. The number of tourists who visit Norway every year is almost as many as the total population of the country.

Vikings settled in Norway nearly 2,000 years ago. They formed a united country in the late 800's. From 1380 to 1814, Norway

Top left: The Midnight Sun. Five exposures have been made. One-third of Norway is north of the Arctic Circle, and there the sun shines at night from May to July.
Below left: Waery Valley. Much of Norway is very mountainous.
Left: Location map of Norway.
Below: The Market Place at Trondheim. The town is situated on the Trondheim Fiord—one of the longest in Norway.

Two churches—one Anglican, one Evangelical—stand side by side on the shores of Mahone Bay, Nova Scotia. In the 1700's many Protestants from France, Germany and Switzerland came to Nova Scotia to practise their faith freely.

and Denmark were united. Then, after the Napoleonic Wars, Norway became part of Sweden. But it soon gained a great deal of independence, and became fully independent in 1905. The country was occupied by the Germans from 1940 to 1945, during World War II. In 1972, Norway was offered the opportunity to join the European Common Market (EEC) but the population rejected the move in a national referendum.

Nottinghamshire (area 844 square miles), an inland county of central England, embraces the remains of Sherwood Forest, home of the legendary outlaw, Robin Hood. Its county town is Nottingham, and its population is 974,500.

Most of the county is undulating, with the land rising to about 600 feet in the south-west. The county is drained by the River Trent and its tributaries. The main crops are wheat, oats and root crops.

The main industries are the manufacture of lace, hosiery, textiles, cigarettes, bicycles and *pharmaceutical* (chemists) products. The largest towns, after Nottingham, are Mansfield and Worksop.

Nova Scotia is one of the provinces of Canada with a coastline on the Atlantic Ocean. About 765,000 people live there. It consists of a long, narrow piece of the mainland extending into the Atlantic. It is joined to New Brunswick by the Isthmus of Chignecto. The province's north-eastern end is cut off from the rest by the narrow Strait of Canso. This part forms an island called Cape Breton Island. The area of Nova Scotia is 21,425 square miles.

Nova Scotia has about 1,000 miles of rugged coastline on the Gulf of St. Lawrence, the Atlantic Ocean and the Bay of Fundy. Halifax, the provincial capital, Sydney, and other large cities are situated on the coast. The province has a relatively mild and humid climate.

Nova Scotia has many wild areas of great beauty. Forests cover more than

This map shows the location of Nova Scotia.

half the countryside. The land is generally low and hilly. The highest spot is in the Cape Breton Highlands. Numerous rivers cut through the land. There are hundreds of lakes, including the large Bras d'Or Lake on Cape Breton Island.

The province has valuable natural resources. These form the basis of its industries. Lumber, used especially for making wood pulp and paper, is provided by the forests. Coal fuels the province's blast furnaces and steel mills. Silver, zinc, copper and lead are mined, too. The surrounding waters abound in lobsters, cod, haddock, and other fishes.

Only a small part of the total land can be farmed. Dairy farms supply the cities. There are also mixed farms, producing crops and livestock. The Annapolis Valley is known for its apple orchards.

In the 1700's, the British gained the region from the French. They named it Nova Scotia, meaning *New Scotland*. Under the French it had been part of the territory they called *Acadia*. The province was one of the original four which joined to form the Dominion of Canada in 1867.

Novel People have told stories from earliest times to entertain each other. These early stories were probably highly coloured versions of historical events, often told in ballad form. The written work of fiction we call the *novel* developed from these beginnings.

IMPORTANT NOVELISTS

Miguel Cervantes (Spanish, 1547-1616) — *Don Quixote*
John Bunyan (English, 1628-88) — *Pilgrim's Progress*
Daniel Defoe (English, 1660-1731) — *Robinson Crusoe*
Jonathan Swift (Anglo-Irish, 1667-1745) — *Gulliver's Travels*
Samuel Richardson (English, 1689-1761) — *Pamela*
Henry Fielding (English, 1707-54) — *Tom Jones*
Laurence Sterne (English, 1713-68) — *Tristram Shandy*
Tobias Smollett (English, 1721-71) — *Roderick Random*
Sir Walter Scott (Scottish, 1771-1832) — *Waverley*
Jane Austen (English, 1775-1817) — *Pride and Prejudice*
Honcré de Balzac (French, 1799-1856) — *Le Père Goriot*
Nathaniel Hawthorne (American, 1804-64) — *The Scarlet Letter*
William Thackeray (English, 1811-63) — *Vanity Fair*
Charles Dickens (English, 1812-70) — *David Copperfield*
Charlotte Brontë (English, 1816-55) — *Jane Eyre*
Emily Brontë (English, 1818-48) — *Wuthering Heights*
Anthony Trollope (English, 1815-82) — *Barchester Towers*
George Eliot (English, 1819-80) — *The Mill on the Floss*
Gustave Flaubert (French, 1821-80) — *Madame Bovary*
Feodor Dostoievsky (Russian, 1821-81) — *Crime and Punishment*
Leo Tolstoy (Russian, 1828-1910) — *War and Peace*
Herman Melville (American, 1819-91) — *Moby Dick*
George Meredith (English, 1828-1902) — *The Egoist*
Mark Twain (American, 1835-1910) — *Huckleberry Finn*
Émile Zola (French, 1840-1902) — *Nana*
Thomas Hardy (English, 1840-1928) — *The Mayor of Casterbridge*
Marcel Proust (French, 1871-1922) — *Remembrance of Things Past*
Joseph Conrad (British, 1857-1924) — *Lord Jim*
Henry James (American, 1843-1916) — *Portrait of a Lady*
James Joyce (Irish, 1882-1941) — *Portrait of the Artist as a Young Man*
Thomas Mann (German, 1875-1955) — *Buddenbrooks*
Franz Kafka (Czech, 1883-1924) — *The Trial*
E. M. Forster (English, 1879-1970) — *Howard's End*
D. H. Lawrence (English, 1885-1930) — *Sons and Lovers*
Scott Fitzgerald (American, 1896-1940) — *The Great Gatsby*
Boris Pasternak (Russian, 1890-1960) — *Doctor Zhivago*
Aldous Huxley (English, 1894-1963) — *Brave New World*
Ernest Hemingway (American, 1898-1961) — *The Old Man and the Sea*
George Orwell (English, 1903-50) — *Nineteen Eighty-Four*
Grahame Greene (English, 1904-   ) — *Brighton Rock*
Mikhail Sholokov (Russian, 1905-   ) — *And Quiet Flows the Don*
William Golding (English, 1911-   ) — *Lord of the Flies*
Patrick White (Australian, 1912-   ) — *Voss*

The framework of the story is called its *plot*. Our attention is usually held by one or two main characters, whose progress we trace to a climax or final outcome. The characters and events are usually depicted like those of real life. The story may be told in the *first person*, as if one of the characters is telling it himself. This limits the writer to describing only those events and thoughts experienced by this character. By 'standing outside' the story, the author can tell

Four important novelists. Above:
George Eliot, Charlotte Brontë. Below:
Thomas Hardy, Henry James.

This apparatus was one of the first *particle accelerators* or 'atom smashers'.

A more powerful type of accelerator for splitting atoms and studying the energy produced was invented by E. O. Lawrence during the 1930's. His apparatus, called the *cyclotron,* used two hollow metal electrodes, each shaped like the letter D. These *dees,* as they were called, were given alternate positive and negative charges by an alternating current. This exerted a 'push and pull' effect on the particles, which whirled around and around in the dees at ever increasing

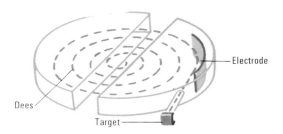

The cyclotron is a particle accelerator or an atom smasher. It accelerates charged atomic particles to high speeds, and the particles are then made to bombard atoms in a target of a metal or some other substance. The reactions caused give scientists information about the structure of the atom. The particle is injected into the cyclotron at the centre of the machine. Electric fields in the dees cause the particle to accelerate. A powerful magnetic field caused by electromagnets situated above and below the dees makes the particle move in a circle. As it increases in speed, it starts to spiral outwards. An electric charge in the electrodes deflects the particle from the dees to hit the target.

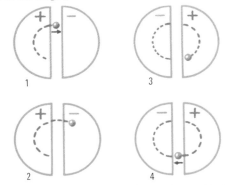

A positively-charged particle is accelerated between the dees towards the negatively-charged dee (1). In the dee (2), it moves at constant speed in a circle. When it again reaches the space between the dees (3), the electric field on the dees is reversed so that the particle is accelerated towards the other dee, which is now negatively charged (4).

us much more. Various time sequences may also be used. The events of the story may be unfolded *chronologically,* in the order in which they happen, or we may be led back and forth in time.

Nuclear energy The nucleus of the atom consists of particles called protons and neutrons, held together by powerful attractive forces. (See Atom.) When the nucleus is broken to pieces, these forces are released as energy in the form of heat and radiation. In 1932 Sir John Cockcroft and E. T. S. Walton 'split' atoms of lithium by 'bombarding' them with alpha particles from a lump of radium. The alpha particles, being positive electrically, were speeded up by being attracted down metal tubes which were charged negatively. At the bottom of the tubes was placed a piece of lithium metal.

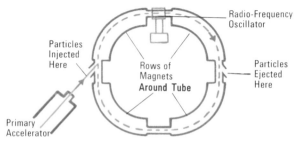

The synchrotron is a more powerful particle accelerator. High-energy protons are accelerated to almost the speed of light in a circular tube. The protons are first accelerated in a smaller accelerator and injected into the tube. A radio-frequency oscillator kicks the protons to higher speeds, and an increasing magnetic field produced by rows of magnets around the tube keeps them in a circular path. On the last circuit, the oscillator causes them to be ejected from the tube to hit a target placed nearby.

speeds, finally 'bombarding' the specimen placed at the exit from the dees.

One of the most modern types of atom smashers is the *synchrotron*. The walls of a circular tube (which can have a diameter of 60 feet or more) are lined with powerful magnets, whose 'field of force' keeps the bombarding particles in the centre of the tube. The particles are whirled around the tube at ever increasing speeds by a high frequency alternating current.

The various substances being bombarded in atom smashers give off particles of different kinds, including alpha particles and beta particles, which can then be studied using an apparatus called the *bubble chamber.*

The particles enter a large tank of liquid hydrogen, which 'boils' into a gas along the path taken by the particles as they pass through the liquid. This path

can then be seen and photographed as a thin line of hydrogen bubbles.

The atoms of certain elements can split by themselves, without the help of bombarding particles in accelerators. The atoms of uranium, for example, can do this. Uranium-235 is an isotope that occurs naturally with the commoner uranium-238.

If a lump of uranium-235 is larger than a certain 'critical size' all its atoms will split in a fraction of a second and enormous amounts of energy will be given off as an explosion. Uranium-235 is used to make atomic bombs.

This *chain reaction,* as it is called, can be controlled in a *nuclear reactor.* A large block of graphite (the kind of carbon used in pencil 'lead') has holes drilled in it. In these holes are placed a number of *fuel rods* which are made of uranium-238 which also contains a small proportion of the 'explosive' atoms of uranium-235. These keep on splitting and giving off energy within the uranium-238 and heat is produced in the graphite block. As the uranium-235 atoms split very fast-moving neutrons are produced. Uranium-238, unfortunately, absorbs fast neutrons, but not slow-moving neutrons. So to keep the 'reaction' going the fast neutrons are slowed down when they pass through the graphite block, which for rather obvious reasons is called a moderator. Now the uranium-238 will not absorb the neutrons, which can freely

Nuclear fission occurs when slow neutrons are captured by nuclei of uranium-235. Fast neutrons have to be slowed by a moderator, such as graphite. The nuclei of uranium-235 split to produce nuclei of *fission fragments,* such as barium and krypton, neutrons and vast amounts of energy as heat.

Fast
Neutrons

Slow
Neutrons

Graphite
Moderator
Slows
Neutrons

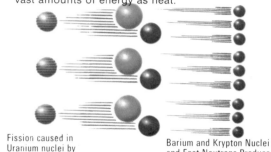

Fission caused in
Uranium nuclei by
capture of Slow Neutrons

Barium and Krypton Nuclei
and Fast Neutrons Produced
as Uranium Nucleus Fissions

move about among the uranium-238 atoms, bombarding them so that they will keep on splitting as a 'controlled' chain reaction.

The heat energy produced by this type of reactor can be harnessed in a nuclear power station. Air or carbon dioxide is pumped around the moderator block, is heated, and then passes into a boiler, where the hot gas changes water into steam. The steam is then piped off to drive steam turbines, which in turn drive generators producing electricity. To stop the reactor working the control rods are fully inserted in the reactor.

Number We use numbers to count and to describe quantity. In prehistoric times, people could probably describe groups of objects only with such imprecise words as *few, several* or *many*. Then, most likely, they began to count on their fingers: 5 on each hand, giving a total of

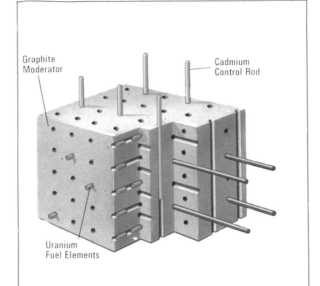

In a nuclear reactor containing uranium fuel and a graphite moderator, the fuel elements are placed in tubes inside the moderator. Cadmium control rods can be moved in or out of the reactor to decrease or increase the amount of heat produced.

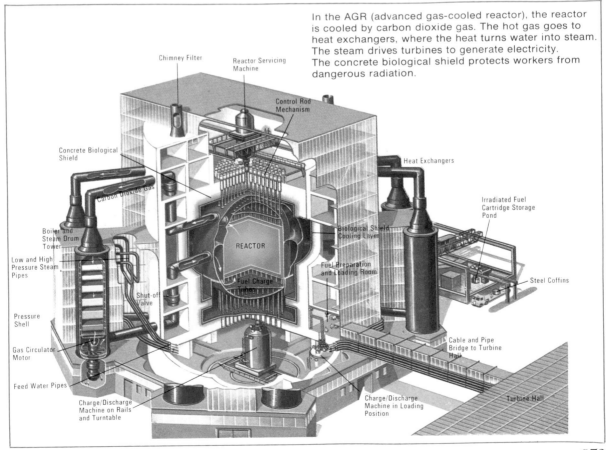

In the AGR (advanced gas-cooled reactor), the reactor is cooled by carbon dioxide gas. The hot gas goes to heat exchangers, where the heat turns water into steam. The steam drives turbines to generate electricity. The concrete biological shield protects workers from dangerous radiation.

10. From this arose the system of numbers built around the quantity of 10. It is the system we use today, and it is called the *decimal system,* from the Latin word *decem,* meaning ten.

In the decimal system, every number can be expressed by using only ten basic digits: 0, 1, 2, 3, 4, 5, 6, 7, 8, and 9. In a decimal number the value of the digits depends not only on their own size, but also on their *position* or *place* in the number. Going from right to left, the places in a number stand for ones, tens, hundreds, thousands and so on. For example, in the number 9037, 7 stands for 7 units or 7×1, 3 for 3 tens and 9 for 9 thousands. The 0 (or *zero*) in the second place tells us that there are no hundreds. It is necessary, because without it we would not know that the 9 means '9 thousands' not '9 hundreds'.

Mathematicians call 10 the *base* of our system. The positions or places corres-

pond to *powers* (multiples) of 10. That is, 10 to the first power (written 10^1) is 10×1 or 10. Then, 10 to the second power (10^2) is 10×10 or 100, and 10 to the third power (10^3) is $10 \times 10 \times 10$ or 1,000.

Although 10 is a convenient base for us to use in everyday life, it is not the only one around which a number system can be built. The ancient Babylonians used 60 as the base of their system, and engineers and scientists today often use a system based on 12, called the *duodecimal system,* or one based on 2, called the *binary system.*

The binary system is very important because it is the only system that a digital computer can use. It has only two digits: 0 and 1. In the computer, 1 can correspond with the flow of an electric current, and 0 with the absence of electricity. In this way, the computer can express any number, no matter how large, simply as a series of on and off pulses of electricity.

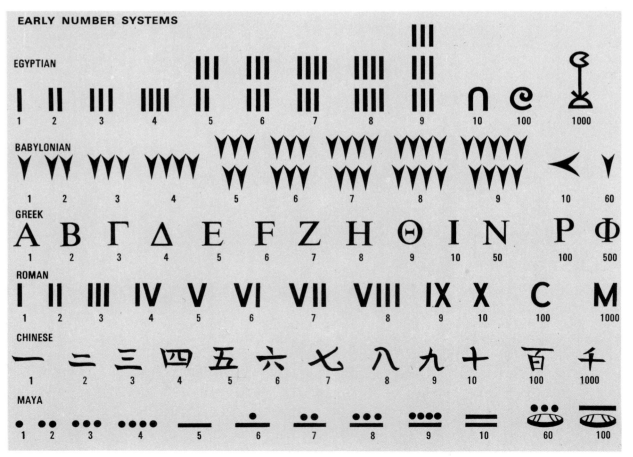

EARLY NUMBER SYSTEMS

In binary numbers, the places stand for powers of 2—that is, they are the 1's, 2's, 4's, 8's places, and so on. The numbers 1 to 8 are written as follows in the binary system: 1, 10, 11, 100, 101, 110, 111, and 1000.

So far, we have been dealing with the *natural numbers,* that is, whole numbers greater than zero. These numbers are infinite—that is, they stretch on for ever. Each of them can be classified as *odd* or *even,* depending on whether it is exactly divisible by two (even) or not (odd). For example, 8 is even, but 9 is odd. Mathematicians call certain numbers, such as 1, 2, 3, 5, 7, 11, 13, 17, and 19, *prime numbers.* These are numbers that cannot be divided by any other number (other than themselves or 1).

Besides the natural numbers, however, there are other kinds, such as *negative numbers,* which are less than zero. We indicate these by putting a minus sign before them. We use *fractions* to represent values greater than zero but less than 1. The symbol 1/2, for example, means 1 divided by 2 (or one-half). In the decimal system, a dot called the *decimal point* is used to separate fractions from whole numbers. The fractions are written to the right of the decimal point, and the place values go in multiples of ten just as they do for the whole numbers. The first place stands for tenths, the second place for hundredths, the third place for thousandths, and so on. For example, 7·5 means 7 and 5 tenths; 7·05 means 7 and 5 hundredths; and 7·005 means 7 and 5 thousandths.

The symbols used for writing down numbers are called *numerals.* In ancient times, people invented many different numeral systems. Some were better than others. The Egyptians, for example, used *hieroglyphics* (picture symbols) to stand for quantity, but they did not discover the use of positions or places.

The Romans thought of a system that used letters to stand for number values: I for 1, V for 5, X for 10, L for 50, C for

Let's imagine we've gone on holiday to Fenland. The people have always used the fingers of one hand for counting—for they only have one arm!

When they get to the last finger, they call this number fen—one complete hand of fingers, just as we use ten to describe our two complete hands. After this they have to start using the same fingers again—fen one, fen two, fen three, fen four. At the last finger they will have two handfuls. This is called two fen.

Here we have three fen three fingers (above). How are these numbers written down? There are no problems with one (1), two (2), three (3), and four (4). But then we come to fen. We need to remember that this is one complete handful and not five fingers. It is written as 10 (one fen and no extra fingers). The other numbers can be written, for example, two fen three—23, or three fen two—32.

When we have a handful of handfuls we need a special name, just as we do for ten tens. We call it a fundred and it is written 100. The next number will be fundred and one (101), fundred and two (102), fundred and three (103), and then fundred and four (104). We can go further and write fundred fen (110), fundred three fen four (134) and so on.

Fundred three fen four is the number:

····· ····· ····· ····· ····· ····· ····· ····· ····

When we go above four fundred four fen four we use fousand (1,000).

The Fenland number system is called a base 5 system, since the only numbers used are 0, 1, 2, 3, 4. All the normal arithmetic problems can be worked out in a base 5 system.

100, D for 500, M for 1000. The numbers were made up of combinations of letters, but again places were not used. Sometimes even today dates are written on buildings in Roman numerals, but for ordinary use the system is too clumsy.

The numerals we use every day are called *Arabic numerals.* They came to Europe from Arabia in the A.D. 800's. But they originated in India hundreds of years earlier. The great advance of the Hindu mathematicians was the idea of 0 or zero, which made their system the most useful invention.

Nursing —that is, caring for sick people and for others in need of help—is today one of the most highly respected professions. But this was not always the case. From the 1600's to the mid-1800's nurses were untrained and were considered disreputable, and hospitals were unhygienic, cold and miserable. At an earlier period, the Church had provided most nursing care through nursing orders of nuns and monks. But during the Reformation many of the monasteries were shut down, and nursing fell into decline.

Modern nursing dates from 1860, when Florence Nightingale opened the first professional training school at St. Thomas's Hospital in London. Her fame as a selfless heroine of the Crimean War did much to improve the reputation of nurses, and people again came to realize the nobility of working for the sick.

Today, nurses perform many important duties apart from nursing the sick back to health. They assist in surgical operations, act as midwives in the delivery of babies, take care of the old, provide public health information and visit the bedridden in their homes. In most countries, nurses must train for several years before they are registered to practise. Their training includes both classroom lessons and practical work in hospital wards.

Nuts are a kind of fruit. They consist of a hard, tough outer shell that covers and protects the seed. Common examples of nuts include hazel-nuts and acorns. The hard covering, or *pericarp,* does not split open to release the seed when the fruit is ripe. Instead, the whole fruit falls from the plant and the germinating seed later breaks through the pericarp. Botanists describe nuts as 'dry, one-seeded, indehiscent fruits'.

Some of the 'nuts' that greengrocers sell are not really nuts at all. The hard shells of the walnut and coconut, for example, develop from the inner layers of the pericarp only, not the whole pericarp as in true nuts. The outer fleshy layer of a

Top: The acorn is a true hard-shelled nut. The horse chestnut (above) is really a seed. One or more glossy brown 'nuts' are contained inside the spiky green capsule.

walnut, and the fibrous layer of a coconut, are stripped off before these 'nuts' are sent to market.

Nylon has been the leading synthetic fibre since the 1940's, when nylon stockings, or nylons, first appeared on the market. It was the original synthetic fibre. Wallace Carothers, an American chemist, first produced it in about 1935.

Nylon is strong, resists wear and rotting, needs no ironing, and 'drip dries'. It is widely used in shirts, socks, and all kinds of clothing, either by itself or mixed with other fibres. In thick filament form, it is used to make fishing nets and strings for tennis racquets.

Nylon is called *synthetic* because it is made wholly from chemicals. It is made by a process called *polymerization,* in which small molecules combine together to form larger ones, called *polymers.* The nylon polymer is called a *polyamide.* Polyamides are suitable for making fibres because their molecules are in the form of long chains.

Nylon is widely used for many products. A section from a 100 foot long Dracone (left) is used to transport oil. It is filled with oil and floated. Nylon is also used to make extremely high quality rope.

Nylon is made by heating in a pressure cooker, called an *autoclave*, a mixture of two chemicals derived from coal tar, petroleum, or natural gas. The nylon polymer is made into fibres by *melt spinning*. It is forced while molten through holes in a *spinneret,* just like all synthetic fibres. (See Fibres.)

O

Oasis is the name given to any fertile area in a desert. Oases vary in size from small clumps of palm trees, with sparse vegetation, to huge areas as big as an English county. Damascus, in Syria, for example, is a city founded in a huge oasis.

The reason for the existence of oases is that rivers around a desert's edge may disappear underground, but they continue to seep through the solid rocks beneath the arid sands. Where the water rises to the surface in springs an oasis occurs. But the water may also be tapped by sinking wells. Desert soil may be extremely fertile, lacking only water.

Oases occur at places in the desert where underground water reaches the surface. The diagram shows how water may seep to the surface along a *fault* (break) in the rock. Oases also occur at places where men have dug wells to tap underground water-bearing rocks.

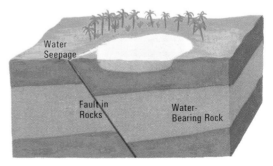

Water Seepage

Fault in Rocks

Water-Bearing Rock

Oases are natural halts for travelling caravans. Two well known caravan centres are the oases at Murzuk, in Libya, and Buraida, in Saudi Arabia. But the greatest oasis of all is in Egypt, where for thousands of years life has depended upon careful use of the waters of the Nile.

Ocean currents are great streams of water moving slowly through the world's oceans. They flow at all levels. Surface currents are caused mainly by winds; deeper currents depend on changes in temperature and other properties of the water.

The main surface currents follow the paths of the prevailing winds. The North and South Equatorial Currents flow westwards parallel with the Equator. Nearer the Poles this water returns eastwards as the West Wind Drift in the Southern Hemisphere and the North Atlantic and North Pacific Drifts in the Northern Hemisphere. All together there are five great circular ocean movements, clockwise in the north, anticlockwise in the south. There are two in the Pacific Ocean, two in the Atlantic Ocean, and one in the Indian Ocean (which lies mainly south of the Equator).

Currents have no definite boundaries, and a slow-moving wide current is often called a *drift*. Ocean currents can greatly affect the climate of the coasts near which they flow. The warm waters of the North Atlantic Drift, washing the coast of north-west Europe warm the winds passing over them and give Norway an ice-free port well within the Arctic Circle. Yet, on the other side of the Atlantic, the cold Labrador Current, sweeping down from the Arctic, gives Labrador a mean January temperature as much as 45 °F below that of Scotland, which has the same latitude, and freezes the coast to the equivalent of southern France.

Deep currents consisting of cold and denser water flow beneath the surface currents. From the North Atlantic a cold deep current flows south to the Antarctic, where it brings plant nutrients to the surface and supports a large animal population, including seals and whales. An even deeper cold current flows back towards the Equator under this Arctic current.

Oceans cover nearly three-quarters of the Earth's surface. Large areas of water are called *oceans,* and they usually separate

The surface currents of the oceans follow prevailing winds. The map of currents in January shows that they form a series of nearly closed loops, which rotate clockwise to the north of the Equator and anticlockwise to the south. In July, the Indian monsoon winds blow eastwards and the monsoon drift changes direction.

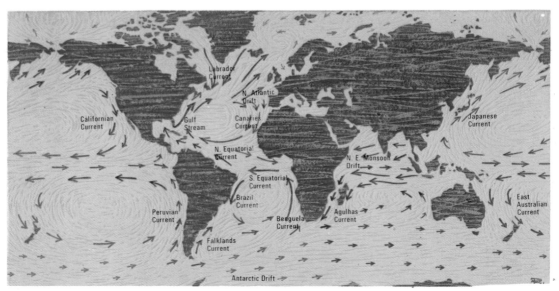

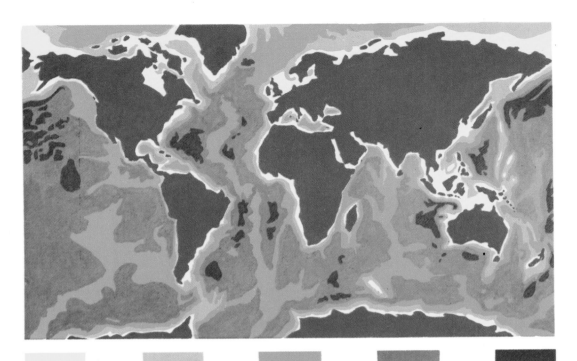

0–600
Feet

600–6,000
Feet

6,000–12,000
Feet

12,000–18,000
Feet

Over 18,000
Feet

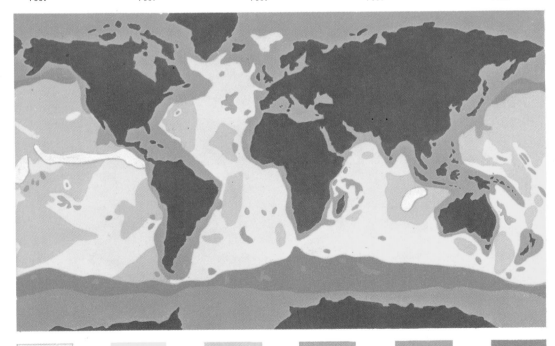

Radiolarian
Ooze

Globigerina
Ooze

Red Clay

Pteropod
Ooze

Terrigenous
Deposits

Diatom
Ooze

The map of the ocean depths, top, shows that great
mountain ranges, such as the mid-ocean ridges, rise
from the ocean floor. Mud, oozes and clay cover the
ocean bed. *Terrigenous* deposits are materials washed
or blown into the sea from the land. Oozes are formed
by the skeletons of tiny organisms, such as *diatoms,
pteropods* and *radiolaria*. Red clay is a mixture of
volcanic dust and such other things as sharks' teeth.

the continents. Smaller areas separating islands or enclosed by land on several sides are called *seas*, *gulfs* or *bays*, *channels*, or *straits*. The waters separating Britain from the mainland of Europe are called the English Channel and the North Sea. The Gulf of Mexico and the Caribbean Sea separate North and South America from the West Indies.

There are five oceans. The Pacific Ocean, between America and Asia, is the largest and deepest, covering a third of the world's surface. It extends one-third of the way around the world at the Equator. The Atlantic Ocean separates America from Europe and Africa. The Indian Ocean is bordered by Africa, Asia and Australia. The Arctic Ocean lies between the land masses around the North Pole, and is covered mostly by ice. The waters around the Antarctic continent are called the Antarctic Ocean, but they do not have bordering land masses like the other oceans.

Around most coasts there is a shelf of land extending out from the coast under the sea. This shelf, called a *continental shelf*, has a depth of up to 600 feet. It may extend for several hundred miles, and then the sea-floor falls steeply away to the ocean bottom or the *abyss*. The abyss is about 12,000 to 16,000 feet deep. It consists of great plains, called *abyssal plains*, crossed by ridges and mountains and by deep trenches. Islands occur where the undersea mountains, often volcanic, break the surface. The deepest known spot on earth is the bottom of the Mindanao Trench off the Philippine Islands in the Pacific Ocean. It is 37,782 feet deep, over seven miles.

The oceans abound in life. Light penetrates the sea down to about 500 feet, and no plants can live below this depth. Thus the upper layer of the ocean and the continental· shelf are rich with animal and plant life. The fish in the upper layer live down to a depth of about 2,000 feet. And below this depth, strange deep-sea fish prowl (see Deep-Sea Fishes).

The ocean is constantly on the move. Waves rise and fall on the surface, caused by the wind. Waves in the open sea are rarely more than about 10 feet high, but in severe storms they may reach a height of more than 100 feet. If such waves reach the shore, they cause great damage. But the most destructive waves are the *tsunamis*, named after the Japanese word for *great wave* and often incorrectly called *tidal waves*. They are not caused by tides or by the wind, but by undersea earthquakes or volcanic eruptions that shake the sea-floor. Tsunamis race across the ocean at great speeds.

Ocean currents are general movements of warm and cold water throughout the world's oceans. There are several great systems of ocean currents, affecting life in the sea and the climates of bordering lands. (See Ocean Currents.)

Oceans began as water came out of the rocks or fell from the sky as rain, when the Earth cooled from its original molten state. It filled great basins formed of heavy rock, surrounding the higher land masses of light rock. The land masses gradually moved apart, eventually forming the continents and oceans in the positions they occupy today. As rivers ran over the land into the sea, they dissolved minerals from the rock.

Man has many uses for the sea. Many people depend on fish and other sea

In many areas, great ocean waves which are caused by the wind provide excellent opportunities for surfing.

animals for food. Useful substances such as iodine and magnesium can be extracted from salt obtained by evaporating sea-water in salt pans. Other useful products from the sea include sponges and sea-weeds. Trade is carried by ships across most of the world's oceans and seas. Men are beginning to harness the tides to produce electricity, and to use nuclear power to extract fresh water from sea-water.

Talking points
* As the world's population grows, Man is using up the resources of the Earth's crust at an increasing rate. Some people believe that in the future Man will have to take much more from the oceans to supply his needs. Discuss the ways in which he might do this.
* Ocean currents have a great influence on the climates of the land near which they flow. Take one of the great circular ocean currents and try to calculate what effect it would have if it suddenly started to flow in the opposite direction.
* Animal life in the ocean exists at different depths. Draw up a chart showing what forms of life live at what depths.

Articles to read
Atlantic; Deep sea fishes; fishes; Indian Ocean; Pacific; Tides.

Octopus An octopus is a sea animal of fearsome appearance. Its eight tentacles, with their rows of suckers, surround a bulbous head containing eyes and a sharp beak. But it is not a dangerous animal. Octopuses are *molluscs,* like the snail and the oyster. Unlike most other molluscs, however, the octopus has no shell.

There are about 150 kinds of octopuses living in all the world's oceans. They vary in size from a few inches across up to more than 30 feet, but the common octopus is about two feet across.

Octopuses live in nooks and crannies in the sea-bed. They are hard to spot because they change colour to merge with their surroundings. The octopus moves by pulling itself along with its suckers, with which it can exert a powerful grip, or by forcing a jet of water out of an outlet called a siphon. The second method shoots the animal backwards.

Octopuses feed mainly on crabs and shellfish, which they catch with their tentacles, poison with a venom produced by glands in the mouth, open with the beak, and clean out with the tongue.

O'Higgins, Bernardo (1778-1842), the hero of the Chilean struggle for independence, ruled Chile from 1817-1823.

Chile decided to fight for independence from Spain when Napoleon overthrew the Spanish king. At first the struggle went badly. O'Higgins, the son of an Irishman who had been governor of Chile, was fired with revolutionary ideals. He joined the Argentinian patriot José de San Martín and they invaded Chile in 1817. By

The suckers of an octopus (left) have thick rims and grow on low mounds of muscle. The cuttlefish and some squids have teeth around their suckers (centre). A few squids have suckers containing retractable claws (right).

The common octopus has an arm-span of about 2 feet. Some octopuses are only a few inches across, but the largest measure more than 30 feet.

1818 the Spaniards were defeated. O'Higgins was forced to abdicate in 1823 by people who opposed his reforms.

Ohio is a state in the midwestern region of the United States. Its name comes from its chief river, the Ohio, which flows along the Kentucky and West Virginia borders in the south. Ohio is an important industrial state and about three-quarters of its 10,652,000 inhabitants are city dwellers. Columbus is the state capital.

Abundant natural resources have helped Ohio's prosperity. Its mineral resources include coal, rock salt, limestone and oil. Iron and steel are manufactured and the state is known for its production of many kinds of machinery. Ohio's large manufacturing cities include Cleveland, Cincinnati, Columbus, Dayton and Akron. Farmers in the state grow maize and soyabeans, and raise cattle and pigs.

Ohio became the 17th state of the United States in 1803. Before the Civil War, it was a leader in the anti-slavery movement.

Oil-bearing plants bear seeds, nuts, or fruits from which useful oils can be extracted by grinding and squeezing the seeds in a press. These oils have many uses. Some of them, called drying oils, absorb air to form a tough film. Drying oils, which include linseed oil, obtained from flax seed, are used to make paints and varnishes. Corn oil, olive oil, ground-

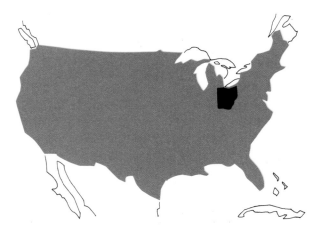

This map shows the location of Ohio.

nut oil and many others are used in the kitchen as cooking oils and in the manufacture of margarine and soap. Many oils obtained from plants are used as flavourings, such as oil of lemon or peppermint. Some oils obtained from fragrant plants are used in perfumes (see Perfume).

Oklahoma is a state in the south-western United States. Rolling prairies cover much of the state, but there are some forests and the south and east are hilly. In the north-west is a narrow strip of land called the 'Panhandle', which is a dry plain. Oklahoma's many large rivers include the Arkansas and the Red River, which forms the boundary with Texas in the south. The largest cities are Oklahoma City, the capital, and Tulsa. The population is 2,600,000.

The state has vast mineral resources, chiefly of petroleum, natural gas, and coal. Its other major source of wealth is farming. Oklahoma is famous for its herds of beef cattle and its wide wheat fields. Factories in the cities process food and manufacture machinery.

Today more Indians live in Oklahoma than in any other state except Arizona. After the United States purchased the region from France in 1803, it designated a large area as a reservation, known as Indian Territory. But from 1889, white settlers were allowed to enter. Oklahoma became a state in 1907. It suffered greatly

A location map of Oklahoma.

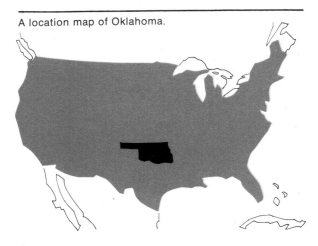

Olives are pulped in a primitive mortar. They are an important crop in Mediterranean countries.

during the Depression of the 1930's. During this period abnormal weather conditions turned much of the land into a barren Dust Bowl, and many farmers left the state.

Olives are the black or green fruits of the olive tree. This evergreen tree, a native of the Mediterranean region, is now widely grown in warm districts in many parts of the world. It reaches a height of nearly 40 feet, and has lance-shaped leaves. The olive tree is very slow growing and lives to a great age. The oldest trees are known to be over 1,000 years old. The small, fragrant flowers are white and funnel-shaped. The fruit resembles a small, fleshy plum. It is one of the oldest cultivated crops and was first grown in Crete about 5,500 years ago.

The wood of the tree is easily worked, and particularly prized for ornamental objects. The olives themselves are edible, and are often pickled and stuffed. They are also widely used in salads and as appetizers. *Olive oil* is a pale yellow oil extracted from the crushed fruits. It is used in salads and as a cooking oil, and also as a lubricant. It is an important ingredient of many soaps, cleaners, and ointments.

Olympic Games This is a gathering of the world's best amateur athletes who meet in friendly rivalry in a variety of tests of prowess based on the ancient games held at Olympia in Greece.

The revival of the Games was initiated by the French Baron Pierre de Coubertin, and the first Games of the modern era took place in Athens on 6 April 1896. It was intended that the Games should take place every four years, but they have been interrupted by two World Wars.

Basketball was one of the most popular and eventful indoor sports of the Olympic Games in 1972.

Modern Olympic Games have subsequently been held in Paris (1900), St. Louis (1904), London (1908), Stockholm (1912), Antwerp (1920), Paris (1924), Amsterdam (1928), Los Angeles (1932), Berlin (1936), London (1948), Helsinki (1952), Melbourne (1956), Rome (1960), Tokyo (1964), Mexico City (1968) and Munich (1972). Separate Winter Olympic Games have been held since 1924.

The XXth Olympiad was held in Munich, Germany in August and September 1972, and 129 countries (the highest number so far) sent their athletes to take part in the sports of Archery; Athletics; Basketball; Boxing; Canoeing; Cycling; Equestrian; Fencing; Football; Gymnastics; Handball; Hockey; Judo; Modern Pentathlon; Rowing; Shooting; Swimming, diving and water-polo; Volley Ball; Weightlifting; Wrestling; Yachting. The games were marred by tragedy, when six members of the Israeli team were kidnapped and held hostage by Arab guerillas who demanded the release of Arabs

held captive in Israel. The athletes were all killed during a rescue attempt made by the West German police.

Gold medals are awarded to event winners, silver and bronze to those placed second and third. The U.S.A. has won most gold medals, and Ray C. Ewry (U.S. high and long jumper 1900-1908) has won the most individual golds—eight. In 1968 Al Oerter (U.S.) won the discus throw event for the fourth successive time. The greatest number of women's golds (four) was won by Francina Blankers-Koen (Netherlands) for sprints, hurdles and relay events in 1948, and Betty Cuthbert (Australia) in 1956 (three golds) and 1964 (one gold). In the 1972 games, Mark Spitz (U.S.) won four individual and three relay gold medals in swimming events. This is a record number of gold medals won in a single celebration of the games. Mark Spitz won two relay gold medals during the 1968 games giving him a total of nine, thus equalling the record held by Paavo Nurmi of Finland.

The Marathon race of 26 miles 385 yards commemorates the epic run of Pheidippedes who in ancient times was said to have run this distance to bear news of a Greek victory over the Persians.

The most coveted prize of the Ancient Games was the Pentathlon, combining long jump, javelin throw, running, discus throw and wrestling. One of the toughest events in the Modern Games is the Modern Pentathlon, consisting of riding, fencing, pistol shooting, swimming and running competitions.

The Olympic Games are conducted by athletes under oath to participate for the honour and glory of sport.

At the first modern Olympic Games held in Athens in 1896, only 300 competitors from 12 nations took part. The 1896 Marathon race was run over the same route that Pheidippedes ran when he brought the news of the victory from the plains of Marathon to Athens. The first modern Marathon was won by a Greek, Spyros Louis.

Omar Khayyám (1050?-1123) was a Persian astronomer and poet. His famous *Rubáiyát*, a series of *rubais* or *quatrains* (four-line rhymes), was translated by Edward Fitzgerald and first published in 1859. The original *Rubáiyát* consisted of independent stanzas, containing the poet's thoughts on the mysteries of life, but Fitzgerald arranged them to show a connected train of thought.

Omar Khayyám was born at Naishapur, in Khorasan. *Khayyám* means *tent-maker* and probably refers to his father's trade. Fitzgerald says in his introduction that Omar Khayyám studied under a doctor of law at Naishapur with Nizam-ul-Mulk and Hasan-ben-Sabbah, the leader of a fanatical sect called the Assassins. The three pledged to help each other in after-life. Nizam-ul-Mulk later became vizier and granted Omar a pension.

Omar became royal astronomer and devised a new Persian calendar, which was probably more accurate than the Gre-gorian one. He also showed his skill as a mathematician in an Arabic book on algebra.

Omnivores are animals that will eat both plant and animal food. Man, for example, is an omnivore. So are such animals as badgers, bears and rats. (See Carnivore; Herbivore.)

This map shows the location of Ontario.

Ontario, with 7,611,000 people, has the largest population of any of the Canadian provinces. It produces more manufactured goods than all the other provinces put together. It also leads in mining and in farming. Ottawa, the capital of Canada, is situated in south-east Ontario.

Most of Ontario's people are of British descent. About one-tenth are descendants of French settlers. About 50,000 American Indians live in Ontario too. They live on reservations.

Ontario has an area of 412,582 square miles. It borders on Quebec in the east, Manitoba in the west, and the United States in the south. Four of the five Great Lakes lie along Ontario's southern boundary. Ships from ports on the Great Lakes have access to the ocean through the St. Lawrence Seaway. Nearly all the people of the province live in the south. This part of the province has the chief industrial cities, including Toronto, Canada's second largest city and the capital of Ontario. The other cities include Hamilton, London and Windsor.

Northern Ontario touches Hudson Bay and James Bay. It is a wild region of woodlands, rivers and lakes. The climate is so cold that few people live there. In some places the ground is permanently frozen. Northern Ontario provides the provinces with valuable resources. They include lumber; minerals, such as copper, gold, iron, nickel, platinum and uranium; fish; and furs.

Ontario's factories produce nearly all Canada's motor-cars. Iron and steel, aircraft, and machinery are other important products. Ontario's farmers raise dairy and beef cattle. They also raise pigs, sheep and poultry. Maize, wheat, rye and vegetables are grown. There are large areas of fruit orchards and tobacco fields.

Chippewa, Huron and Iroquois Indians inhabited Ontario before French explorers, fur traders and missionaries arrived in the 1600's. Britain won Ontario from France in 1763, following the French and Indian Wars. Ontario was one of the original four provinces that formed the Dominion of Canada in 1867.

Opera is a musical play in which the music is more important than the words. People often distinguish between *grand opera*, in which the story is serious and every word is sung, and *light opera* (sometimes called *operetta, comic opera,* or *opera buffa*), in which the story is light-hearted and some of the dialogue is spoken.

Opera has a number of *conventions* or customs which distinguish it from ordinary theatre. Most operas begin with an *overture,* a piece for orchestra. In addition to the principal characters, there is usually a chorus. The action of the play is often held up for a song.

The principal solo songs in operas are often called *arias.* In most operas of the 1600's and 1700's, an aria is preceded by a *recitative,* a passage in which the singer declaims words to music.

Music and drama have been closely linked for thousands of years, but opera as we know it today began in Italy during

Above: Joan Sutherland, the Australian soprano, in Donizetti's opera *Lucia di Lammermoor.* This is one of her most famous roles.

Bottom: A production of *Der Meistersinger von Nurnberg,* at the famous festival in Bayreuth, Germany, of Richard Wagner's works.

the 1590's. The first great opera was *Orfeo* (1607) by Claudio Monteverdi. Other great opera composers of the 1600's included the Italian Alessandro Scarlatti and the Frenchmen Jean Baptiste Lully and Jean Philippe Rameau.

Italian opera became very formal and undramatic in the 1700's, but a German,

Christoph Willibald Gluck, linked story and music more closely. His example was followed by Wolfgang Amadeus Mozart with works such as *The Magic Flute*.

Most of the operas performed today were written in the 1800's. In Italy, one of the greatest opera composers was Giuseppe Verdi (e.g. *Aida; Rigoletto*). Other leading Italians included Vincenzo Bellini *(Norma)* and Gioacchino Rossini (e.g. *The Barber of Seville)*. In Germany, Richard Wagner wrote a series of great musical dramas in which music, story and characters were created together (e.g. *Tannhäuser; The Mastersingers*).

Important opera composers of the 1900's include Richard Strauss (e.g. *Elektra),* Alban Berg (e.g. *Wozzeck*) and Benjamin Britten (e.g. *Peter Grimes*).

Opossum An opossum is a primitive pouched mammal, one of the group known as *marsupials* (see Marsupials). Opossums are the only marsupials that live in North America. They also live in South America and on the islands of the Caribbean. Opossums vary in size from larger than a cat to the size of a mouse. They are furry, with pointed, rat-like faces, and long, often naked tails. New-born opossums are tiny, and live and grow for a long time in their mother's pouch. After leaving the pouch, they ride on her back

for several weeks. When attacked, opossums pretend to be dead, hence the expression, 'playing possum'.

Oracle This was a place where the ancient Greeks came to consult their gods about the future. There were a number of these places, each one believed to be sacred to a different god or goddess. If a worshipper visited the oracle at Delphi, for example, he would ask the priest to discover from the god Apollo either what he could expect to happen, or what he should do next. The priest would conduct a ceremony which involved going into a kind of trance. After some time, he would announce the god's advice. This was usually worded in a mysterious fashion, and the worshipper had to think carefully in order to figure out its meaning.

Orange Free State is a province of the Republic of South Africa. Its capital is Bloemfontein, and its population is 1,386,000.

The province is a high, grassy plateau crossed by a series of low ridges. It lies between the Vaal and the Orange rivers.

The common opossum (left) and the woolly opossum (right) are both marsupials—animals with pouches.

The oracle at the temple of Apollo, an ancient Greek god, at Delphi. People went there to get advice on such matters as war and peace or personal problems.

The Orange Free State was settled by the Boers (Dutch farmers) in the early 1800's. It is mainly an agricultural province. This road leads to Antelope Park, Golden Gate.

Below: Location map of the Orange Free State.

To the north is the Transvaal; Natal and Lesotho lie to the east; and the Cape Province borders it on the south and south-west. The principal rivers, apart from the Orange and Vaal, are the Modder and Caledon.

The Orange Free State is primarily an agricultural province. Vast quantities of livestock, especially sheep, are reared, and maize, wheat and fruit are cultivated. Gold production is on the increase, with the major goldfield located at Odendaalsrus. There is diamond mining around Jagersfontein, and coalmining at Coalbrook. A large chemical industry has been built up at Sasolburg, where the extraction of oil from coal is a thriving industry.

The first *Boers* (Dutch farmers) began to settle north of the Orange River about 1820. After a period of British rule, the Orange Free State became independent in 1854. It became a province of the Union of South Africa in 1910.

Orchestra is a large group of musicians playing many kinds of instruments. Groups of musicians playing only a few kinds of instruments (generally brass and percussion) are usually called *bands*.

The *symphony orchestra* may contain more than a hundred players. It is arranged by sections of instruments (see Musical instruments). The strings account for about two-thirds of the players and sit at the front of the orchestra. The violins are usually seated in two groups (first and second). The woodwinds are usually in the middle behind the violas. The brass, few in number but loud in volume, are usually at the back to one side, while the percussion section is at the back to the other side. Solo performers such as pianists, violinists, or singers are always at the front by the conductor, who has complete control of this vast array of musicians.

A symphony orchestra is the largest kind of orchestra. Some composers write pieces for strings only, and a string orchestra usually contains about thirty players. If a few woodwind or other players are added, the orchestra is generally called a *chamber orchestra*. The small orchestras in theatres are known as *pit orchestras* because they play in the pit in front of the stage. They usually consist of strings, a few woodwind and brass players, and a percussionist.

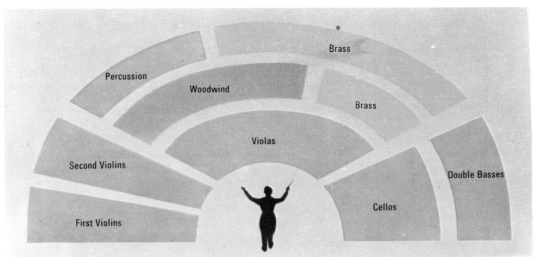

Symphony orchestras usually consist of more than 100 musicians. Two-thirds play stringed instruments.

In jazz music, a large group is made up of a brass section of trumpets and trombones, a section of saxophones, and a *rhythm section* of piano, double bass, and drums. This group is often called a *big band*, and most *dance orchestras* or *dance bands* are made up like this. A *modern jazz orchestra* contains instruments such as flutes and vibraphone to produce a more varied sound. A *variety orchestra* or *light orchestra* is usually a big band with a large string section.

The *gamalan orchestra* of south-east Asia consist almost entirely of percussion instruments such as xylophones, gongs, and chimes.

Orchids are a large group of plants that grow chiefly in tropical areas. Orchids are all perennial herbs. Kinds that live in temperate regions grow in the normal manner with their roots in the soil. But several tropical species grow as *epiphytes* on the trunks and branches of trees. Their roots are especially adapted to absorb water directly from the humid atmosphere, but they do not take any food from the trees on which they grow.

Orchid flowers vary enormously in size, shape and colour. Many forms resemble certain insects—perhaps to lure insects to pollinate their flowers. Their colours range from white through greens and browns to dark purplish-reds, and their size from less than half an inch to eight inches across.

Some orchids bear their pollen in two gluey bundles that stick to the heads of insects searching for nectar. They are thrust intact onto the stigma of the next orchid the insect visits.

Many orchids grow wild either on the ground or from the trunks and branches of trees. But gardeners also grow many varieties. The orchids below are *Orchis morio* (left) *Ophrys sphyodes* (centre) and *Cypripedium calceolus*.

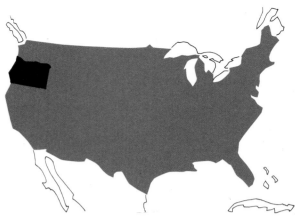
This map shows the location of Oregon.

Oregon is a Pacific coast state of the United States. Forests cover more than half its area, and make it a leader in timber production. Rivers provide hydro-electric power, and their waters are rich in fish, particularly salmon. The rugged mountains of the Cascade Range divide the state into rainy western and drier eastern regions. The state capital is Salem.

More than half of Oregon's 2,091,000 people live in the Willamette valley in the north-west. This area has the state's major cities — Portland, Salem and Eugene — and the leading industries. Timber-based industries, such as plywood and paper production, are the most important. Others include food processing and machinery manufacture. Rolling farm-lands in Oregon produce valuable wheat, fruit and vegetable crops. Livestock rais-ing and dairying are also important.

European navigators first sailed along the Oregon coast in search of the North-west Passage between the Atlantic and the Pacific. Many settlers reached the state in the 1840's from the east by means of the Oregon Trail. They fought fierce wars with the Indians. Oregon became a territory in 1848, and a state in 1859.

Organ is a keyboard instrument in which sound is produced by air vibrating in pipes. These may number up to 33,000 and range from quarter of an inch in length up to 64 feet. An organ may have several keyboards, one above the other and a pedal keyboard for the feet. *Stops* are drawn out to bring different sets of pipes, each producing different qualities of sound, into play. By using these, a large variety of sounds can be obtained. An electric fan blows the air into the pipes when the keys are pressed.

In the *reed organ* or *harmonium,* the feet pump bellows that blow air over reeds. In *electronic organs,* the sound is amplified by a loud-speaker.

Orkney and Shetland Islands are two Scottish island counties to the north-east of Scotland.

Orkney comprises more than 70 islands, of which 26 are inhabited. The county town is Kirkwall on Mainland (or Pomona), the largest island, and the population of the county is 17,000. The nearest island to the mainland is South Ronaldsay, about 6 miles across the Pentland Firth.

The *Shetlands* (Zetland) are made up of about a hundred islands. The county town is Lerwick, and the population is 17,500. The principal islands are Mainland, Yell, Unst and Foula. The main industries on these bleak, infertile, nearly tree-less islands are agriculture and fishing. Their tiny Shetland ponies are world renowned; and Fair Isle has become famous for its intricately patterned knitwear.

Osaka is Japan's second largest city. It is one of a ring of cities surrounding Osaka Bay on the mainland of Honshu. Many canals and streams of the Yodo River run through the city, with numerous bridges crossing them.

Most of Osaka's 2,980,000 people work in industry. Shipbuilding and the pro-duction of steel, machinery, cotton and other textiles and chemicals are major activities. There are many banks and a stock exchange. The rebuilt castle, origin-ally dating from the 1500's, is a landmark.

During Japan's feudal period, the city developed as a centre of trade. Today nearby Kobe handles more shipping.

The late Neolithic settlement of Skara Brae in the Orkneys was built around 1500 B.C. It is outstanding for the completeness of its preservation. Orkney is very rich in prehistoric remains.

Oslo is Norway's capital and largest city. It stands at the top of the 65-mile-long Oslo Fiord, on the south-eastern coast of Norway. Oslo's port is ice-free, and handles most of the country's shipping. Wood, wood products and fish are the main exports. Factories in the city produce processed foods, paper, chemicals and machinery. The population of the city is 487,000.

Oslo's fine buildings include Akerhus Castle, the royal palace, and the university. Among its other attractions are the statues by Gustav Vigeland in Frogner Park. Much of the land within the city limits is still forest and open countryside. The original city of Oslo, founded in 1048, burned down in 1624. It was rebuilt by the Danes as Christiania, and kept that name until 1925.

Osmosis is a process by which water or some other *solvent* passes from a dilute solution to a stronger or more concentrated one when the two are separated by a *semi-permeable membrane*. Such a membrane allows the small molecules of solvent to pass through, but it holds back the larger molecules of the dissolved substances.

Osmosis can be explained by the fact that the molecules are always moving about and bumping into the membrane. Solvent molecules hitting one of the microscopic pores in the membrane would pass through to the other side. They would move in both directions, but the greater concentration of solvent molecules in the dilute solution means that more of them pass through from that side than from the other. There is thus a net movement of solvent from the dilute solution to the stronger one. During this process the dilute solution becomes stronger (because it is losing solvent) and the concentrated solution becomes weaker. In theory, the process would go on until the two solutions were of equal strength. This does not always happen, however, because pressure builds up on one side of the membrane and prevents more solvent from entering.

Osmosis can be demonstrated quite easily by filling a long-stemmed thistle funnel with sugar solution and covering the end securely with a piece of Cellophane. If the funnel is then up-ended in a beaker of pure water the water will pass through the Cellophane and the level will rise in the stem of the funnel.

Osmosis is vitally important in living things, for living cell membranes are nearly all semi-permeable. The water and salt balance of cells is maintained by this process. Plant roots also absorb water by osmosis. The water in the soil is a much weaker solution than the sap in the plant, and water thus passes in through the fine walls of the root hairs.

Otago is a province at the southern end of New Zealand's South Island. Including the Southland region, it has an area of 25,530 square miles. Over 286,000 people live in Otago, many of them in Dunedin and Invercargill, the two largest cities. Both cities are served by nearby ports.

Otago's land is low along the eastern coast. In the south and central regions are plateaus and plains with rich pastureland. The Southern Alps extend into the province in the north and there are other high and beautiful areas in the west. Here the action of prehistoric glaciers created finger-shaped lakes and dramatic fiords (deep inlets of the sea).

Otago's economy depends primarily on sheep farming. Meat and wool are the chief exports. Fruit and wheat are grown, and forests in the province provide lumber and pulp for paper-making. Hydroelectric schemes on the Clutha and Waitaki rivers produce power.

Permanent settlement of Otago began in 1848, when ships sponsored by the Free Church of Scotland arrived at what is now Dunedin. In the 1860's, the discovery of gold brought prosperity to Otago.

Ottoman Empire was a Muslim empire that began in Asia Minor about 1290. Its founder was a warrior called Osman, from whom the empire took its name. He was the leader of a Turkish tribe living under the protection of the Seljuks. The tribe declared itself independent and, by a series of dazzling conquests over the years, came to replace the vast Byzantine Empire.

In 1453, the Ottoman Turks captured Constantinople. The empire reached its peak during the reign of Suleiman the Magnificent (1520-1566). By the end of the 1500's it extended eastwards from Serbia and Hungary into Kurdistan and Mesopotamia, and parts of Arabia. It stretched from the Black Sea region southwards as far as Sudan.

Turkish sea power was largely destroyed by the Christian League at the Battle of Lepanto (1571). The Turks had failed to invade Italy or capture Vienna, despite repeated attempts. By the end of the 1900's, the Ottoman Empire was forced out of existence by the expansion of Russia towards the Black Sea.

Ottawa (pop. 536,000) is the capital city of Canada. It is situated on the River Ottawa in the province of Ontario, 100 miles west of Montreal. Elegant public buildings in the well-laid-out city include Parliament House, with its tall Tower of Peace, the National Museum, an art gallery, two cathedrals, and a university. Ottawa is an important centre of the lumber trade and manufactures machinery, flour and paper. The Ottawa River and its tributaries are used to transport the lumber, which is floated downstream. The Chandière Falls nearby are used to provide hydroelectric power.

Otter The otter is a flesh-eating mammal that lives in and near water. Otters are related to badgers and weasels. They have

Opposite: A 16th-century miniature showing the Ottoman Sultan Orhan presenting a bow to the Egyptian Ambassador. The Ottoman Empire produced many superb works of art.

The fur of otters is soft, warm and valuable. Otters use their tails as rudders when swimming.

thick-set bodies and short legs with webbed toes. They grow to a length of about four feet. They are superb swimmers.

River-otters live in burrows in riverbanks, and eat fish, frogs, snails, and other water creatures. Sea-otters live in the coastal waters of the North Pacific. They eat crabs, sea-urchins, and shellfish, but not fish.

Owls are birds of prey that hunt mainly at night. There are more than 500 kinds of owls living in all sorts of climates: hot, warm, and cold. Their large heads, flat faces, and forward-looking eyes are very different from those of other birds, and make them easily recognisable.

Owls have hooked beaks, partly hidden in their feathers, and feathered legs and feet that end in powerful claws. Their large eyes give them a thoughtful expression. Rats and mice are their chief prey, and they hunt them with noiseless flight.

Because of the nature of their prey, owls swallow large chunks of bones, skin, and fur with their meat. They have no teeth and cannot digest this matter, so it is channelled to a muscular part of the stomach called the *gizzard*. There, all these indigestible bits are bound together with fur and feathers and brought up through the bird's mouth in the form of pellets. Owls nest in holes in buildings, trees, or on the ground.

The Barn Owl (above) is 15 inches long. The Great Horned Owl (left) is 25 inches in length.

The 24-inch-long Snowy Owl hunts in the Arctic.

Oxford is a cathedral city, university, market, and county town of Oxfordshire, in southern central England. It is situated on the Thames, just over 50 miles west-north-west of London, and has a population of 108,600.

Oxford is best known for its university, the oldest residential university in the United Kingdom. It was established as a centre of learning in the 1100's. University College, the earliest existing college, was founded in 1249. Today there are 39 colleges and halls. Many of the college buildings are superb examples of their period. They include Gothic masterpieces such as the Old Library at Merton College, Magdalen College, and Christ Church; the Sheldonian Theatre designed by Wren in the Renaissance style; and magnificent 18th-century architecture represented by Queen's College.

The most interesting architecture outside the university is the Saxon tower of St. Michael's Church and the remains of a Norman castle and city walls.

Industry received a great boost with

An aerial view of Oxford showing the magnificent old buildings of the University colleges. Besides being a famous university city, Oxford is an important centre of industry, especially of motor car manufacturing.

the establishment of Lord Nuffield's motor car factories in the suburb of Cowley in 1912.

Oxfordshire (area 750 square miles) is an agricultural county in the southern Midlands of England. Its county town is Oxford, and its population is 380,800.

Most of the county is drained by the Thames, which flows along its southern border. A spur of the Cotswold Hills rises in the west, and the Chiltern Hills are prominent in the south-east.

Farming is the main occupation. Barley, oats, wheat and root crops are widely cultivated. Dairy farming is important, but most cattle are reared for beef. Many sheep are also kept.

Oxford is a university town and a major road and rail junction. It is an important motor car manufacturing centre, and also specializes in printing and publishing. Banbury is a busy market town, and Witney produces textiles and blankets. There are cement works at Chinnor.

Oxygen is the most important of all gases to living things. Animals and plants alike need to breathe the oxygen in the air in order to remain alive.

Mammals take in oxygen through the lungs. From there, the blood carries it to all parts of the body. The body 'burns' its food in this oxygen to provide energy and heat. Carbon dioxide is produced by this 'burning' and is carried by the blood to the lungs, where it is breathed out. This process is called *respiration*. Plants, too, respire through their leaves, but during the day, they also take in carbon dioxide and give off oxygen by another process. This interchange of oxygen and carbon dioxide is an important natural cycle.

Oxygen is by far the most abundant chemical element. As a gas, it makes up one-fifth of the air around us. Most of the remainder is nitrogen. Combined with other elements it makes up half of the Earth's crust, and combined with hydrogen almost nine-tenths of the oceans.

When oxygen combines with other

elements, the process is called *oxidation*. Combustion, or burning, is fast oxidation, and rusting is slow oxidation.

Oxygen is obtained commercially by distilling liquid air. Liquid oxygen itself, which is very, very cold ($-183°C$), is used as a propellent for rockets. In gaseous form it is used widely in industry in gas torches (*oxyacetylene* and *oxyhydrogen*) for cutting and welding metals.

In medicine, oxygen is given to patients who have difficulty in breathing. Aircraft and submarines must carry supplies of oxygen for breathing, too.

P

Pacific The Pacific, the largest and deepest ocean in the world, covers an area of 63,802,000 square miles. It is divided into the North and South Pacific Oceans by the Equator. The North Pacific separates the continents of Asia and North America, and the South Pacific separates Australasia from South America.

The trade winds, carrying cool air towards the Equator, and the westerlies, carrying warm air towards the poles, cause the water to circulate clockwise in the North Pacific and the opposite way in the South Pacific. The trade winds blow steadily from the north-east in the northern hemisphere and from the south-east in the southern hemisphere.

The trade winds vary so little that sailing ships relied on them to blow them on course, on their trading routes across the ocean. The Pacific is now crossed by both air and shipping routes between the great continents of America, Asia and Australasia.

Most of the Pacific islands lie within the tropical zone. Because of the climate the main crops grown are sugar, copra, timber, coffee, cocoa and tropical fruits. Owing to the volcanic origin of some of the islands, large deposits of gold, bauxite (aluminium ore), and phosphate are found there.

The many islands in the Pacific can be divided into two geological types. The *volcanic islands,* which are mountainous and heavily wooded, and the low-lying *atolls,* which are surrounded by a ring of coral enclosing a lagoon.

The Pacific islands vary greatly in size, the largest being New Guinea, covering an area of over 300,000 sq. miles. Among the smallest are those of the Ryukyu Archipelago, in the north-west Pacific, south of Japan, which are merely summits of a submerged mountain chain.

Few of the Pacific islands are independent. The majority are administered by either Britain, Australia, New Zealand, France, or the United States. Mostly unpopulated, there are many thousands of islands but they often lie thousands of miles apart.

Polynesia, the biggest group of islands, is widely scattered over the southeastern Pacific. The group includes the Society Islands, the chief one of which is Tahiti, the Tuamotu Archipelago, the Cook Islands, the Leewards, Australs, Marquesas, Pitcairns, Rapas, Gambiers and Easter Island.

Colourful traditional dancing is a popular tourist attraction on the beautiful island of Tahiti.

Fiji, a group of volcanic islands, the largest of which are Viti Levu and Vanua Levu, lies a thousand miles north of New Zealand. To the east of Fiji are the Tonga, or Friendly, Islands, and to the north lie Samoa and the Union Islands.

The Gilbert and Ellice group consist of five widely scattered island territories which are crossed by both the Equator and the International Date Line. They are the Gilbert, Ellice and Phoenix groups, Ocean Island, and the detached islands of Fanning, Washington and Christmas. Separated from Australia by the Coral Sea are two volcanic island groups known collectively as Melanesia. The Solomons, the large group, includes Bougainville, Guadalcanal, Isabel, Malaita, San Cristobal and the Santa Cruz Islands. The New Hebrides group includes Espiritu Santo, Malekula, Eromanga and Efate. To the south lie the Loyalty Islands and New Caledonia.

New Guinea, the second largest island in the world, lies to the north of Australia. Papua, the eastern region of New Guinea, is separated from the Solomons by the Bismarck Archipelago and the Louisiade and D'Entrecasteaux Islands.

Micronesia, a group of small islands in the west Pacific, lies to the north of Melanesia and New Guinea. Most of the islands are unpopulated, and the largest groups are the Marshalls and the Carolines, which are important for their mineral deposits of bauxite and phosphates.

The Philippines, situated in the western Pacific, are separated from Vietnam by the South China Sea. The two largest islands in the group are Mindanao and Luzon, on which is the Philippine capital of Quezon. About 1,500 miles east of Quezon are the Mariana Islands, the largest of which is Guam.

Hawaii, centre of the Pacific air and trade routes, lies 2,000 miles south-west of California. Honolulu, the Hawaiian capital, is situated on the island of Oahu, and close by is Pearl Harbor, headquarters of the United States Pacific Fleet. Hawaii is the 50th state of the United States.

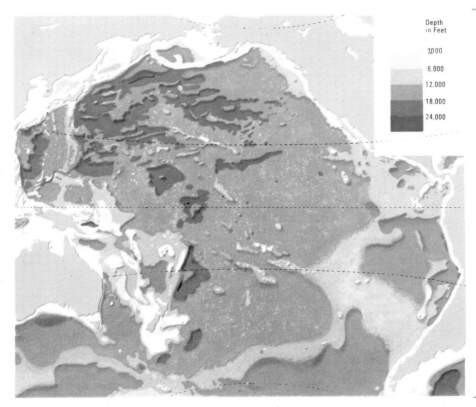

Depth in Feet
3,000
6,000
12,000
18,000
24,000

The vast Pacific Ocean contains the deepest of all ocean trenches, the bottoms of which are more than seven miles deep. Many volcanoes rise from the bed of the Pacific and often form mountainous islands. Other islands were built of the remains of tiny animals called coral polyps. Earthquakes sometimes rock the ocean bed and cause powerful tidal waves called *tsunamis*. These waves travel at great speed and batter coastal areas, destroying much property and drowning many people.

Painting and painters To represent objects or figures on a flat surface (such as stone, wood, or canvas) by applying colours is known as painting. Men have always been impelled to depict objects, people, animals, or even ideas (gods, for example) in this way — the earliest known examples being the paintings on the walls of caves. Examples of primitive cave paintings exist which show a high degree of skill. Such paintings often represent only hunting scenes. Many thousands of years later, frescoes and decorations for dwellings appeared.

After the rock paintings of primitive man had evolved into the frescoes of the Byzantine period, Giotto, of the Middle Ages, broke through the formal ideas of the Byzantine period to paint human beings in a warm and natural way. He laid the foundation on which the works of the Siena school was based, and his great successor was Fra Angelico, with his painting of *The Annunciation*. Later came Botticelli with his great pictures of *Spring* and the *Birth of Venus*.

During the Renaissance, the early 15th century painters made picturesque and infinitely varied paintings. Among these painters were Raphael, Leonardo, and Michelangelo.

The great Venetian school produced such masterpieces as Giorgione's *Sleeping Venus*, while in Germany the work of Albrecht Dürer and Hans Holbein was supreme.

In the 17th century the Bolognese school was founded, with the aim of selecting the finest qualities of the painters who had gone before them. Carracci, Tiepolo, and Canaletto were among the great names, and in Spain, Velasquez achieved great fame with his portrait of Philip IV of Spain.

El Greco, a Cretan who began painting in the middle of the 16th century has become known as the father of modern painting despite the fact that his work was done many years ago.

The 18th century in England saw the

Giotto (1266?-1337, Italian) — *Mourning of Christ*
Jan van Eyck (1386?-1440, Flemish) — *The Arnolfini portrait*
Fra Angelico (1387-1455, Italian) — *Annunciation*
Uccello (1397-1475, Italian) — *Rout of San Romano*
Masaccio (1401-1428, Italian) — *Madonna and Child*
Piero della Francesca (1416?-1492, Italian) — *Baptism*
Giovanni Bellini (1430?-1516, Italian) — *Madonna of the Meadow*
Sandro Botticelli (1444-1510, Italian) — *Primavera*
Hieronymus Bosch (1450?-1516, Flemish) — *Ship of Fools*
Leonardo da Vinci (1452-1519, Italian) — *Mona Lisa*
Albrecht Dürer (1471-1528, German) — *Adoration of the Magi*
Michelangelo (1475-1564, Italian) — *Creation of Adam*
Titian (1477-1576, Italian) — *Portrait of a Man*
Raphael (1483-1520, Italian) — *School of Athens*
Hans Holbein (1497?-1543, German) — *The Ambassadors*
Tintoretto (1518-1594, Italian) — *Origin of the Milky Way*
Pieter Bruegel (1525?-1569, Flemish) — *Hunters in the Snow*
El Greco (1541?-1614, Spanish) — *Burial of Count Orgaz*
Peter Paul Rubens (1577-1640, Flemish) — *Chapeau de Paille*
Frans Hals (1580?-1666, Dutch) — *Laughing Cavalier*
Nicholas Poussin (1594-1665, French) — *Bacchanal*
Anthony van Dyck (1599-1641, Flemish) — *Charles I of England*
Velasquez (1599-1660, Spanish) — *Surrender of Breda*
Claude (1600-1682, French) — *Cephalus and Procris*
Rembrandt (1606-1669, Dutch) — *The Night Watch*
Jan Vermeer (1632-1675, Dutch) — *Artist in his Studio*
Antoine Watteau (1684-1721, French) — *Gilles*
William Hogarth (1697-1764, English) — *The Shrimp Girl*
J. B. S. Chardin (1699-1779, French) — *The Reading Lesson*
Thomas Gainsborough (1727-1788, English) — *Mr and Mrs Andrews*
Francisco Goya (1746-1828, Spanish) — *Parasol*
William Blake (1757-1827, English) — *God Creating Adam*
J. M. W. Turner (1775-1851, English) — *Interior at Petworth*
John Constable (1776-1837, English) — *Brighton Beach*
Edouard Manet (1832-1883, French) — *La Musique aux Tuileries*
Edgar Degas (1834-1917, French) — *L'absinthe*
James A. M. Whistler (1834-1903, American) — *Little White Girl*
Paul Cézanne (1839-1906, French) — *Vieille au Chapelet*
Claude Monet (1840-1926, French) — *Madame Gaudibert*
Pierre Renoir (1841-1919, French) — *The Umbrellas*
Paul Gauguin (1848-1903, French) — *Ia Orana Maria*
Vincent van Gogh (1853-1890, Dutch) — *Sunflowers*
Georges Seurat (1859-1891, French) — *Une Baignade*
Toulouse-Lautrec (1864-1901, French) — *At the Moulin Rouge*
Wassily Kandinsky (1866-1944, Russian-born) — *Bright Picture 1913*
Henri Matisse (1869-1954, French) — *La Desserte*
Georges Rouault (1871-1958, French) — *The Three Judges*
Piet Mondrian (1872-1944, Dutch) — *Composition with Red, Yellow and Blue*
Paul Klee (1879-1940, Swiss) — *A Girl's Adventure*
Pablo Picasso (1881-1973, Spanish) — *Guernica*
Georges Braque (1882-1963, French) — *Guitare et Pichet*
Oskar Kokoschka (1886- , Austrian) — *Polperro, Cornwall*
Marc Chagall (1887- , Russian-born) — *The Reclining Poet*
Grant Wood (1892-1942, American) — *American Gothic*
Jackson Pollock (1912-1956, American) — *Painting 1952*
Sidney Nolan (1917- , Australian) — *Glenrowan*

rise of the great satirical paintings of Hogarth, which were a bitter commentary on his society, and also those of Sir Joshua Reynolds, and Gainsborough, whose elegant paintings are familiar to this day. Constable eventually revolutionized landscape painting, and Turner was among the first to depict the shifting, insubstantial, qualities of light and air.

In the 18th century the elegant paintings of Watteau and Fragonard depicted the mannered life of pre-Revolutionary France. During the 19th century the harsh realism of the Spanish painter Goya contrasted with the French classicism of David, and the Romanticism of Prudhoun and Delacroix.

Eventually, many artists began experimenting with styles and techniques, and the great Impressionist movement finally emerged. This was based partly on the invention of new chemical colours which permitted an entirely new approach to painting. The invention of the photograph drove many painters to the abstract style of painting.

This picture by the Australian artist Sidney Nolan is called *Camp Antarctica.*

Portrait painting has long been popular among artists. Several artists, particularly Rembrandt, painted self-portraits. Sometimes they were commissioned to paint important people of their day. Paintings may commemorate events, such as Van Eyck's picture of the marriage of Giovanni Arnolfini. Religion has greatly influenced artists, including Botticelli and El Greco, whose mystical paintings have great power. Legends, such as that of the judgement of Paris, have also been popular. The landscapes of John Constable and Grant Wood on the opposite page reveal differing approaches to the painting of scenery. Cézanne's *Still Life* reveals the artist's concern with shapes and light.

Self portrait at the Age of 34 by Rembrandt

Portrait of Philip IV by Velasquez

The Judgement of Paris by Rubens

A detail from *Madonna and Child* by Titian

The Young Schoolmistress by Chardin

Still Life with Water Jug by Cézanne is reproduced by courtesy of the Tate Gallery. *Stone City* by Grant Wood is reproduced by courtesy of the Joslyn Art Museum, Omaha. All the other paintings on these two pages are reproduced by courtesy of the National Gallery.

Still Life with Water Jug by Cézanne

The Marriage of Giovanni Arnolfini and Giovanna Cenami by Van Eyck

Mystic Nativity by Botticelli

Adoration of the Name of Jesus, El Greco

Detail from a painting
by Gainsborough

The Haywain by Constable

King Charles I by Van Dyck

Stone City by Grant Wood

*A Young Woman standing
at a Virginal* by Vermeer

Paints We paint our homes both to make them more attractive and to protect them from the weather.

When we decorate, we may apply the paint by brush or by roller. We often give the surfaces both an undercoat and a top coat. The undercoat is generally a *flat* (dull) and the top coat a *gloss* (shiny) paint. In industry paint is generally applied by spraying, which is much quicker.

The colour or whiteness of a paint comes from a powder, or *pigment*. The substance which carries the pigment and dries to a hard film is called the *vehicle*, or *binder*. It contains *solvent*, or *thinners*, to make it easy to apply.

Oil-based paints have a vehicle of an oil and a resin. Most of them are now made from synthetic resins, such as polyurethanes. *Emulsion* paints have a vehicle of tiny droplets of oil or resin in water. Application is therefore much cleaner than with oil paints. *Jelly*, or *non-drip* paints contain a substance which prevents paint from dripping and spilling during application.

Pakistan is an Asian country on the coast of the Arabian Sea. Iran and Afghanistan border it to the west, China to the north and India lies to the east. The country was, until 1971, known as West Pakistan. East Pakistan, which has now become Bangla Desh, is an area of Bengal, more than a thousand miles away across Indian territory. The two Pakistans were created when India became independent from British rule in 1947. The two areas are mainly Muslim, while the rest of India is Hindu. To prevent religious conflict between the two faiths, the British made the Muslim areas into a separate state.

The main languages of Pakistan are Urdu and English. Much of the country is made up of deserts and rugged mountain regions. The Himalayas rise in the north, and Kashmir in the west and the borders with Afghanistan are also mountainous.

Most Pakistanis are farmers. Their chief crops are wheat and cotton. Pakistan's known mineral deposits are not great and its manufacturing industries are small in proportion to the country's size and population. Like India, it has good roads and railways.

Facts and Figures
Area: 310,403 square miles.
Population: 64,400,000.
Capital: Islamabad.

Top: The mosque is a common sight in Pakistan. Most Pakistanis follow the Muslim religion.

Left: A location map of Pakistan.

Bottom: The Khyber Pass is a rugged route connecting Pakistan with its neighbour Afghanistan.

Pakistan has had a troubled history. In 1965, disputes with India over the Kashmir border led to war. In the late 1960's, the Bengalis of East Pakistan began to demand independence from the dominance of the less populous Western region. In 1971, President Yahya Khan prevented the new Pakistani parliament, in which the Eastern region had won a majority, from taking office. Sheikh Mujibur Rahman, the Bengali leader, was arrested and an army was sent to the East to crush the independence movement. India intervened on the side of the East Pakistanis and in the following war defeated the army of West Pakistan. East Pakistan was proclaimed the Republic of Bangla Desh and Sheikh Mujibur Rahman became its first president.

Palaeontology is the study of fossils — the remains of plants and animals which lived millions of years ago but are now extinct. It is a useful science because it tells us about the conditions on Earth long ago, and can help to discover oil and coal. (See Fossils; Prehistoric animals.)

Palm is a tropical or subtropical tree or shrub with a single trunk crowned by a thick cluster of large leaves. The trunk or main stem varies from 2 or 3 to 150 feet in height. There are more than 1,200 species, some of which are very valuable commercially. Among these are the coconut, sago, date and oil palms. By far the most important of them is the coconut palm. The 'milk' or juice of the nut makes a refreshing drink; the white meat or flesh of the nut provides food, oil and *copra* when dried; and the husks, trunk and leaves are used for ropes, matting, building materials and fuel.

Palomar, Mount, in California in the United States, is the site of the Palomar Observatory. This observatory has the world's largest telescope — the Hale Telescope. This instrument has a 200-inch reflector (saucer-shaped mirror). It can

Harvesting dates. Palm trees grow in tropical and subtropical regions and their valuable crops include coconuts, dates and oils.

photograph galaxies (collections of stars) that are millions of light years away from the Earth. The telescope took almost 20 years to construct, and cost over $6 million. It was first used in 1947.

The observatory also has another telescope — the Schmidt Telescope. This instrument has a 48-inch reflector. It has a wider angle than the Hale Telescope, and can gather information from a larger section of the sky. But it has less range.

The observatory on Mt. Palomar is situated 5,600 feet above sea level. It is jointly run by the California Institute of Technology and the Carnegie Institution.

This map shows the location of the Panama Republic.

Panama is a republic in Central America. The Panama Canal cuts across the centre of the country. The canal links the Atlantic and Pacific oceans. The canal and the surrounding Panama Canal Zone are controlled by the United States. West of Panama is Costa Rica, east of it is Colombia. Forests and hills cover much of Panama. But there are lowlands along its coasts. Its area is 29,209 square miles.

Panama's 1,428,000 inhabitants are mainly *mestizos* — people of mixed European and American Indian descent. Spanish is the official language. Most people live by farming or fishing. Rice, sugarcane and bananas are the leading crops. Shrimps, oysters and tuna fish are the main fish catches. Panama's industries, including the manufacture of clothing and furniture, are centred in Colón and in the capital, Panama City.

The Spanish gained control of Panama

in the 1500's. They held it until 1821. Then Panama broke away from Spain and became part of Colombia. It became fully independent in 1903. In the 1950's and 60's there were riots against the continued American domination of the Canal Zone.

Panama Canal The Panama Canal links the Atlantic and Pacific oceans across the Isthmus of Panama in Central America.

The 50-mile long canal is a vital link in the world's shipping routes. Without it, ships would have to sail round Cape Horn at the tip of South America to pass between the Atlantic and Pacific Oceans. This would involve an extra journey of about 8,000 miles.

The construction of the canal was a great feat of civil engineering. It involved damming a river to form a 32-mile-long lake; excavating a 9-mile-long cutting through solid rock; and building three sets of locks to take ships from the sea, up to lake level, and down again.

A French company started work on the Canal in 1881. It was headed by Ferdinand de Lesseps, who had built the Suez Canal twelve years before. But in 1889, the company went bankrupt after completing only a quarter of the project. In 1903, the new state of Panama gave the United States sole, permanent use of a 10-mile-wide canal zone. A year later, American engineers resumed work on the canal. It was completed in 1914. About 55,000 workmen died during the construction of the canal, mainly from tropical diseases.

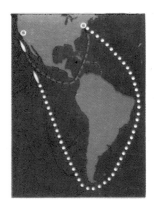

An elaborate system of lock chambers enables ships to pass through the Panama Canal. Each lock chamber is 70 feet deep, 110 feet wide and 1,000 feet long. The map shows how the canal saves a journey of 8,000 miles for ships sailing between the eastern and western coasts of North America.

Pandas are mammals belonging to the Carnivores (the flesh-eating group), although they actually feed almost entirely on plant material. They are related to the racoons (see Racoon). There are two kinds of pandas, the lesser (or red) panda and the giant panda. Both live in Asia.

The giant panda is extremely rare, both in the wild and in captivity. It is the size and shape of a bear, weighing up to 300 pounds, but it is only distantly related to bears. It has bold black and white markings and flat, padded feet. It lives in the bamboo forests of central China, and feeds almost solely on young, green bamboo shoots.

The lesser panda is about 3½ feet long, including the thick, bushy tail, and weighs about 12 pounds. It is chestnut red in colour, with dark bands on its tail. Its face is white with brown markings. It lives at a height of 6,000 to 12,000 feet, on the tree-covered slopes of the Himalayas and other Asian mountain ranges.

Pangolin The pangolin is a curious-looking mammal that is sometimes called the scaly anteater. Its back is covered from head to tail in hard, overlapping scales, rather like those of a pine-cone. Its underparts are, however, soft. When in danger, the animal coils up so that the scales protect it. The pangolin has a long tail, strong claws, and a narrow, pointed head. At the tip is a small mouth. It has no teeth but a long, rope-like tongue, which it uses to catch ants and termites, its main food. Pangolins live underground and come out only at night. Some kinds grow up to six feet in length. They live in Africa and Asia.

Paper in more or less the form we know it today was first made in A.D. 105 by a Chinaman, Tsai Lun. He discovered that certain plant materials could be broken down into fibres (of cellulose) and pressed into a sheet which made a good writing material.

Until the mid-1800's most paper was

The lesser panda (left) lives in hollow trees, coming down to feed on roots, bamboo shoots and other plants. The rare giant panda of central China holds bamboo with a kind of sixth claw on its front paws.

The pangolin curls up when it is threatened by an enemy. Its scales protect it against attackers.

hand-made from rags or from grasses such as hemp and esparto. But then it was discovered how paper could be made from wood-pulp.

Wood-pulp is produced mainly from soft-wood trees such as fir, pine, and spruce. The felled trees are cut into logs and transported, often by water, to the pulp-mills. There they are first debarked in a revolving drum. Then they are broken down into a pulp either by grinding or by boiling with chemicals in

1005

a pressure cooker called a digester. Chemical digestion is used to produce rag and esparto pulp, too.

Groundwood, or mechanical pulp, is used mainly for newsprint—the paper on which newspapers are printed.

The pulp may be pressed into sheets for transport to the paper-mill. There, the sheets are converted back into a wet pulp in a big tub (the hydropulper). The wet pulp then passes to a beating machine, which frays the fibres.

At the 'wet end' of the paper-making machine, the watery pulp is spread over a wire-mesh belt. Most water drains or is sucked away to leave a damp paper web.

The web is then pressed into a firm sheet by heavy rollers and dried by being passed over a series of heated cylinders. Finally, *calender presses* (heavy, heated rollers) give the paper a smooth finish.

Different grades of paper are made by blending various pulps and by varying the amount of beating in the heating machines—the more beating, the denser the paper. High-quality printing papers

are coated with materials such as clay to give them a glossy surface. Some papers are *sized* (treated with glue) to make them take writing better. Tissue papers are given their texture by being scraped off the drying cylinders.

Papyrus is a water plant similar to sedge. It grows on the banks of the Nile and the Ancient Egyptians used the fibrous stem of the plant to make a kind of paper on which they wrote with a pen made from rush. They had red and black inks. Our word 'paper' comes from papyrus. The papyrus plant grew all over the Nile Delta. Its stalk was used to make ropes for ships' rigging. Its root, or rhizome, made a food. Other ancient peoples wrote on clay tablets. Papyrus was much more convenient; so the Egyptians wrote more than the Sumerians, for example. Their writings, which are also called papyrus, survived in great quantity because the climate of Egypt is very dry. This is why we know so much more about Egyptian life than that of other ancient peoples. You can see papyrus in many museums.

Parachute A parachute is a means of falling through the air safely from a great height. Looking rather like a large

Constant inspection of the complicated machinery in a paper mill is necessary to produce high quality paper.

The diagram shows how paper is made from timber. It may take the timber of 7,000 trees to make enough wood pulp for 400 tons of paper. But this amount may be used in one edition of a newspaper.

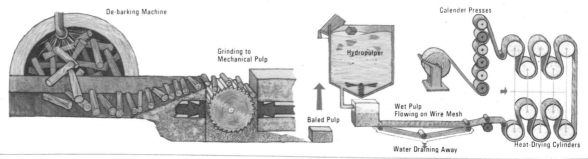

De-barking Machine
Grinding to Mechanical Pulp
Hydropulper
Calender Presses
Baled Pulp
Wet Pulp Flowing on Wire Mesh
Water Draining Away
Heat-Drying Cylinders

Parachutes are important in war. A cluster of six parachutes (top) supports a 2½ ton army truck. Peacetime uses of parachutes include the sport of sky-diving (below). Six airmen join hands in mid-air during a dive.

aircraft or 'drag' racing cars. And they are used in the sport of sky-diving. Special steerable parachutes allow people to control their fall and land accurately on target. Many countries have parachute jumping teams which compete in international matches.

Parachutes are packed in a special way and worn on a harness. A ring on the front of the pack connects with the ripcord. When the ring is pulled, the parachute billows out. The person then falls at a speed of about 16 feet per second.

Paraguay, a republic in South America, is bounded by Brazil, Argentina and Bolivia. It has no coastline. The Paraguay River divides the country into two regions. East of the river is a hilly region, with many long river valleys. There are also swamps. West of the Paraguay River, the land is flat and forest-covered. This region is part of the Gran Chaco of central South America. The area of Paraguay is 157,047 square miles. The capital is Asuncion. Paraguay's 2,400,000 people are mainly *mestizos* — people of mixed European and American Indian descent.

The people grow such crops as cotton, sugar-cane and tobacco for a living. Most farmers earn only enough to feed their families. Food products, textiles, soap and shoes are among Paraguay's manufactures. Rivers are the most important means of transport.

The Spanish began to form settlements in Paraguay in the 1500's. In 1811 Paraguay broke from Spanish rule and became an independent nation.

umbrella, it works by air resistance. The large inverted curved surface moves downwards slowly because of the resistance of the air pressing up against it. For the same reason a leaf or a sheet of paper falls much slower than a stone does.

Today parachutes have four main uses. They are used in emergencies by airmen after they have jumped or been ejected from aircraft and by paratroopers for landing safely. They are used for slowing down the fall of cargoes dropped from aircraft or space capsules after they have re-entered the Earth's atmosphere. Parachutes are used as brakes by high-speed

This map shows the location of Paraguay.